INTRODUCTION

When growing up, I never viewed my parents as compatible. Along with many others who knew and loved my Mom, I will always think of her as a "saint." My father, on the other hand was much more self-consumed, tight with his money and strict. My Mom, Marian, loved and gave unconditionally. When it came to my Dad, Tony, there always seemed to be strings attached --- for me anyway.

I see now that being raised by their two different personalities along with their very different qualities was beneficial for me. Not too much of a good or bad thing... just the right balance. Though it did feel unfair to me back then.

But this book isn't about me. It's about the seven-decade love affair between my (incompatible) Mom and Dad. Either I was terribly wrong about the incompatibility idea or they were living proof of the axiom that "opposites attract".

I first remember seeing the artwork (published in this book) at my Dad's Memorial. My brother and sister-in-law brought it all in a shopping bag. I remember thinking it wasn't being preserved in a manner deserving. I don't recall saying anything about its preservation but the next time I saw all of it --- a few years afterwards --- it was neatly organized in a photo album with sticky pages and velum. Hmmm.

My Dad passed away in 2008 after being diagnosed with dementia more than 6 years earlier. My Mom experienced cardiac arrest one night and passed away in 2003. Toward the end of my Mom's life, the doctors wanted to put my father in a nursing home but my Mom wouldn't have anything to do with that. Already hampered with a heart condition, she was warned that the stress and work involved in taking care of him would result in her dying before him. Sure enough, they called it correctly.

So here I am, 62 years old and the youngest of 3 brothers (each of us born 3 years apart) when I became interested in my Dad's artwork, especially his hand-made, hand-drawn loving cards that served as expressions of his love for my Mom. What I find especially intriguing is that the majority of these cards were created and sent from overseas during World War II. Mom was at home, in familiar surroundings and Dad, was in a strange far-a-away land, with the sound of gunfire and hand grenades exploding in the background. They couldn't have been in two more different places.

When studying Dad's artwork, I soon realized just how much love and affection Dad had for Mom. He absolutely adored her. (Though this was quite evident even during their many post-war years together.) And though his sentiments expressed on paper through simple ink, marker and watercolors passed in one direction, I know with certainty that Mom's love for Dad was equal to his. Or, Mom's love may have even surpassed his. But it's futile (and silly) to try and measure love.

So, this is a love story expressed through a creative, special gift my father was blessed with... the ability to visualize his life and life around him through the images his artful right hand would create. So much of his early work focused on his most obvious and deepest passion, my Mom. World War II separated them for over 3 years immediately after marrying. It must have seemed like an eternity to them.

BACKGROUND

Dad was of Italian decent, arriving at Ellis Island with his family as a two-year-old in 1921. Mom was one year younger. Her family was here in the U.S. much earlier and was primarily of German/Irish descent. Both Mom and Dad were raised as Roman Catholics. Mom would eventually be the first non-Italian to marry into the Grande family. (Once again, proof of the theory that "opposites attract.")

Were there any objections to the marriage among my paternal grandparents (or for that matter, among my maternal grandparents)? I only know that my grandparents always acted like they adored Mom. Sadly, Mom's parents past away before I ever knew them.

THEIR ROMANCE BEGINS

I can't help but think of their first date much like The McFly's "Enchantment Under The Sea" school dance in the movie, "Back to the Future." Their seminal date, "The Prom" is recorded on the first card we know of that Dad created for Mom.

Would their futures and their progeny's futures... or even their very existence (including me of course) have changed if this event didn't happen? Don't know... but thankfully I don't have the formidable challenge of having to go back in time to make sure it happens.

The date of their High School Prom, which took place in our hometown of Astoria, Queens, New York was Friday, May 13, 1938. Take note all you sufferers of triskaidekaphobia out there... their next 55 years were anything but unlucky.

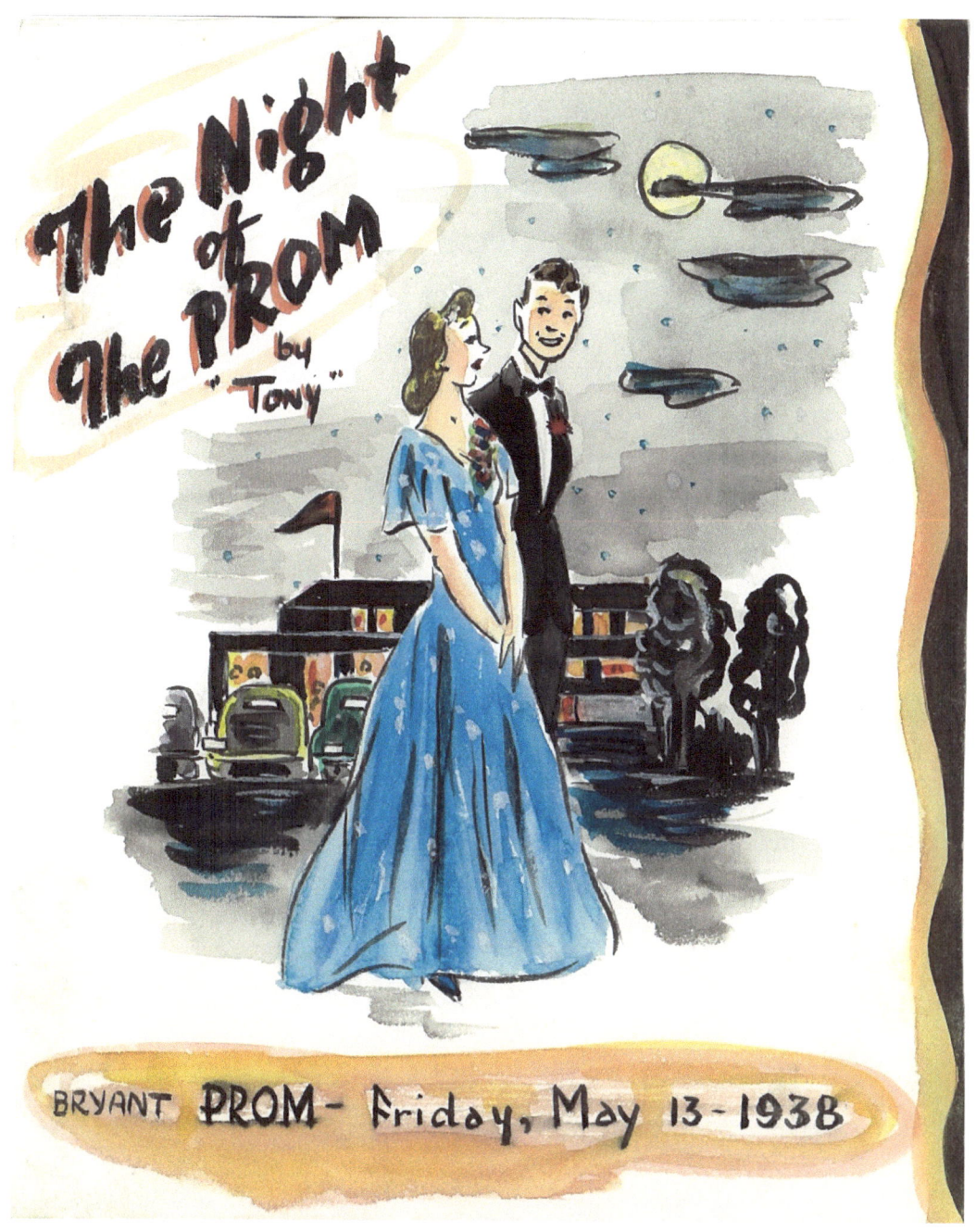

BRYANT PROM - Friday, May 13 - 1938

My research indicates that there truly was a full moon as drawn (the very next night), so I give Dad credit for near perfect lunar accuracy. And I will say with near perfect certainty that they didn't have any idea that 4 years later they'd be married and Dad would be at war over seas.

As Dad did from time to time, there's an original poem included with this card. It was typewritten...

```
THE NIGHT OF THE PROM

I'll never forget, how thrilled you seemed,
And your eyes gleamed, THE NIGHT OF THE PROM.

I'll always remember, that you looked grand
I held your hand, THE NIGHT OF THE PROM.

It was the first time, that I wore a tuxedo,
You had on a gown that made you look so—beautiful.

We danced 'till dawn, and then we walked,
Not one of us talked, the moon was above,

WE fell in love, that wonderful night,
THE NIGHT OF THE PROM.
```

Dad was a far better artist than poet, but I'm sure Mom wasn't as critical as I and loved every word. Though I will say the sentiment sounds so genuine and sincere.

Incidentally, my two older brothers also went to Bryant High School in Astoria, Queens. And, another quick aside --- a scene from the movie, "Bronx Tale" was shot right in front of Bryant High School. And, strangely enough, all the "Bronx Tale" location shooting took place in Queens!

FIRST EASTER CARD

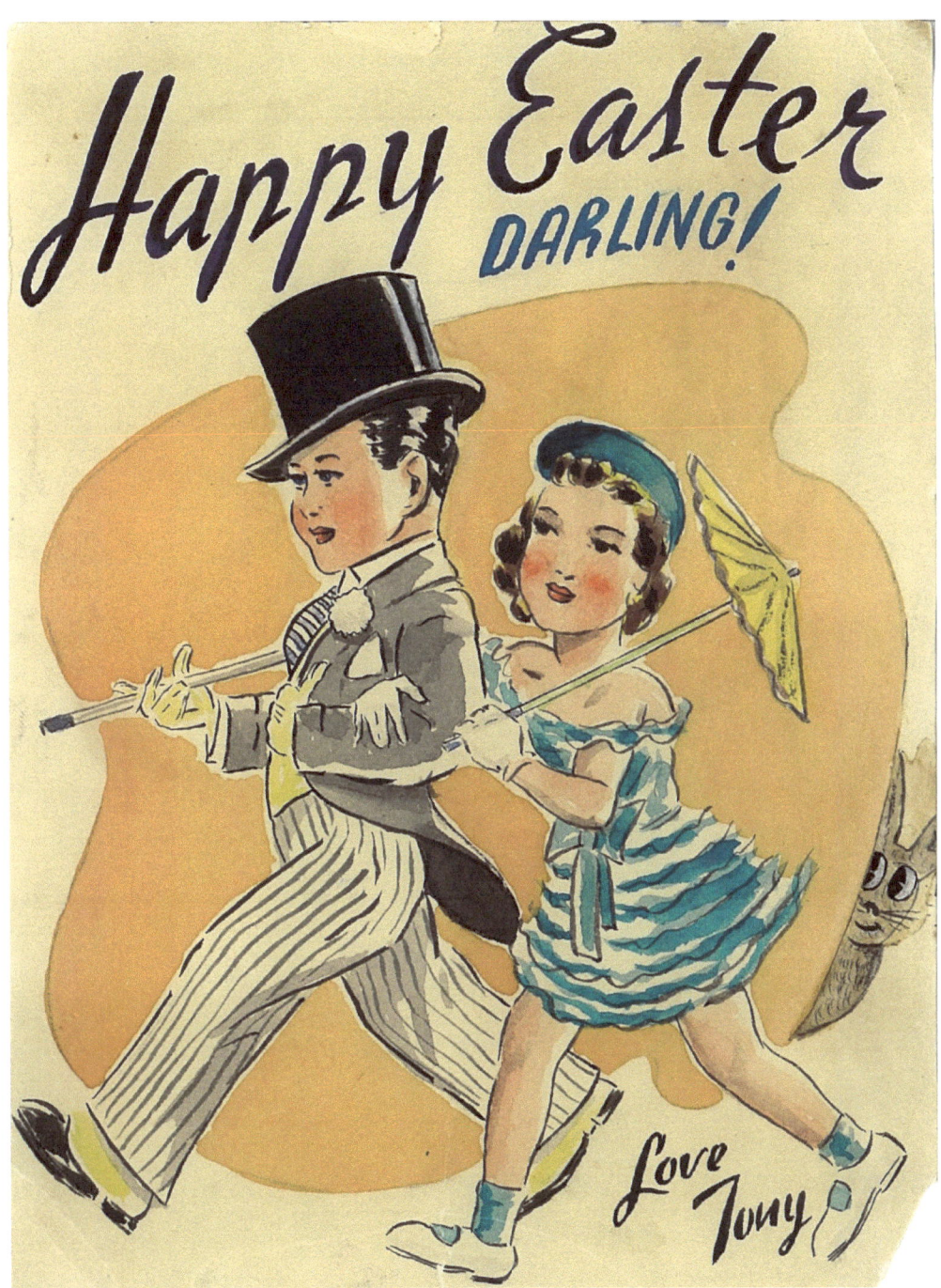

One of my favorites! This early pre-war, pre-marriage card (circa 1939-1940) is the first of Dad's Easter Greetings to Mom. The style is unlike the majority of Dad's subsequent artwork. Their romance, like spring during Eastertime was in full bloom.

There's such innocence depicted in this Easter Greeting. (Did you notice the bunny rabbit timidly but happily peeking out?) Are they children dressed as adults? Or adults dressed as children?

That's one of the things I find so engaging about this card. Again, they both had to be totally unaware of what was waiting for them in only a few short years. The innocence would sadly end (albeit temporarily) with the imminent outbreak of World War II.

MOM'S FIRST CHRISTMAS CARD

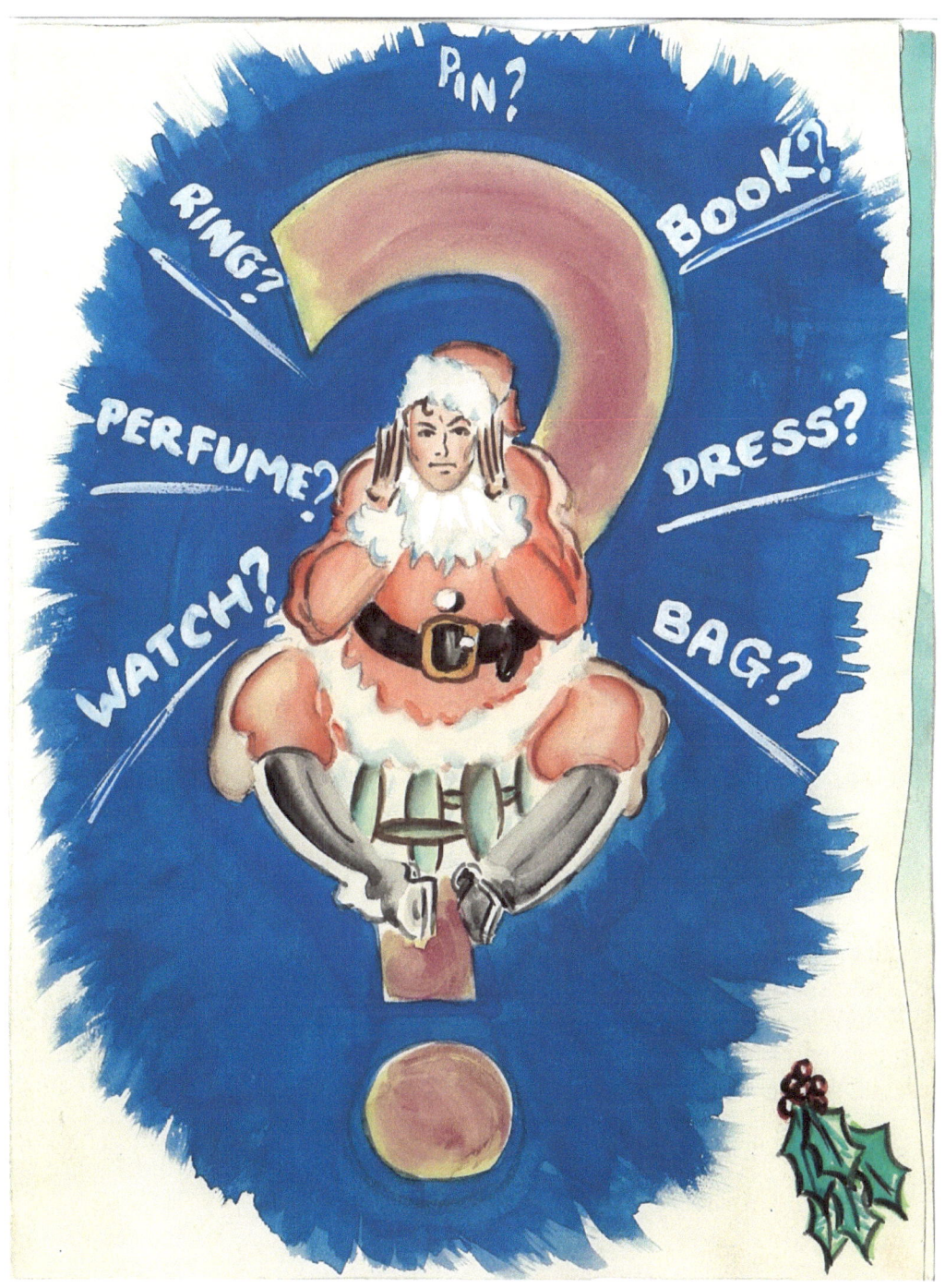

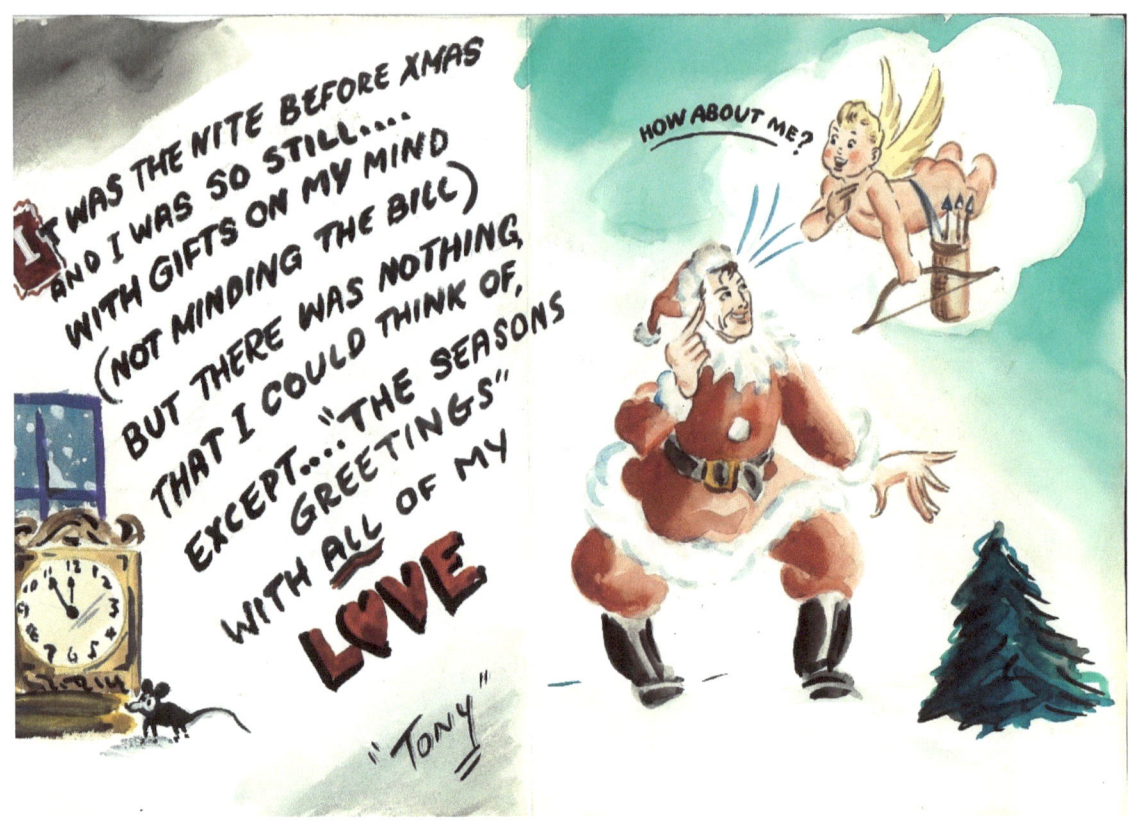

What a clever way of getting out of buying a Christmas gift for Mom! "What a rascal," my Mom might have said! And this is not the only time Dad encountered a momentary lapse of gift giving inspiration... as you will see later. Was he broke? Was he feeling cheap? No time to shop? Would a personalized card be so special as to devalue anything impersonally manufactured, bought and put under the tree? Personally, my answer depends on the day and my mood.

However, the day and the mood have little effect on my thinking that Dad would have liked a second try at the bowed legs he inadvertently (I'm surmising) put on himself. Perhaps he was too nervous wondering if his ingenuity would get him off the hook to concentrate appropriately on his legs... or after that awesome cupid he drew, he relaxed just a little too much. (I love that cupid!)

Nevertheless, I think his brainstorm to have Cupid ask Dad, "What about me?" (as the present) was genius! (Guess my mood is quite favorable to Dad today.)

MOM'S SECOND EASTER CARD

This is probably the most simple and elegant of his love cards to Mom. I'm always surprised when I see Dad's religious references since I can't remember him ever waxing poetic about religion. Mom took us boys to church until we felt old enough to rebel and stop (or play hooky). When we stopped attending church, so did she. Though Mom was spiritual in her own way, she went to church for us. Mom ALWAYS put Dad and us before her own needs.

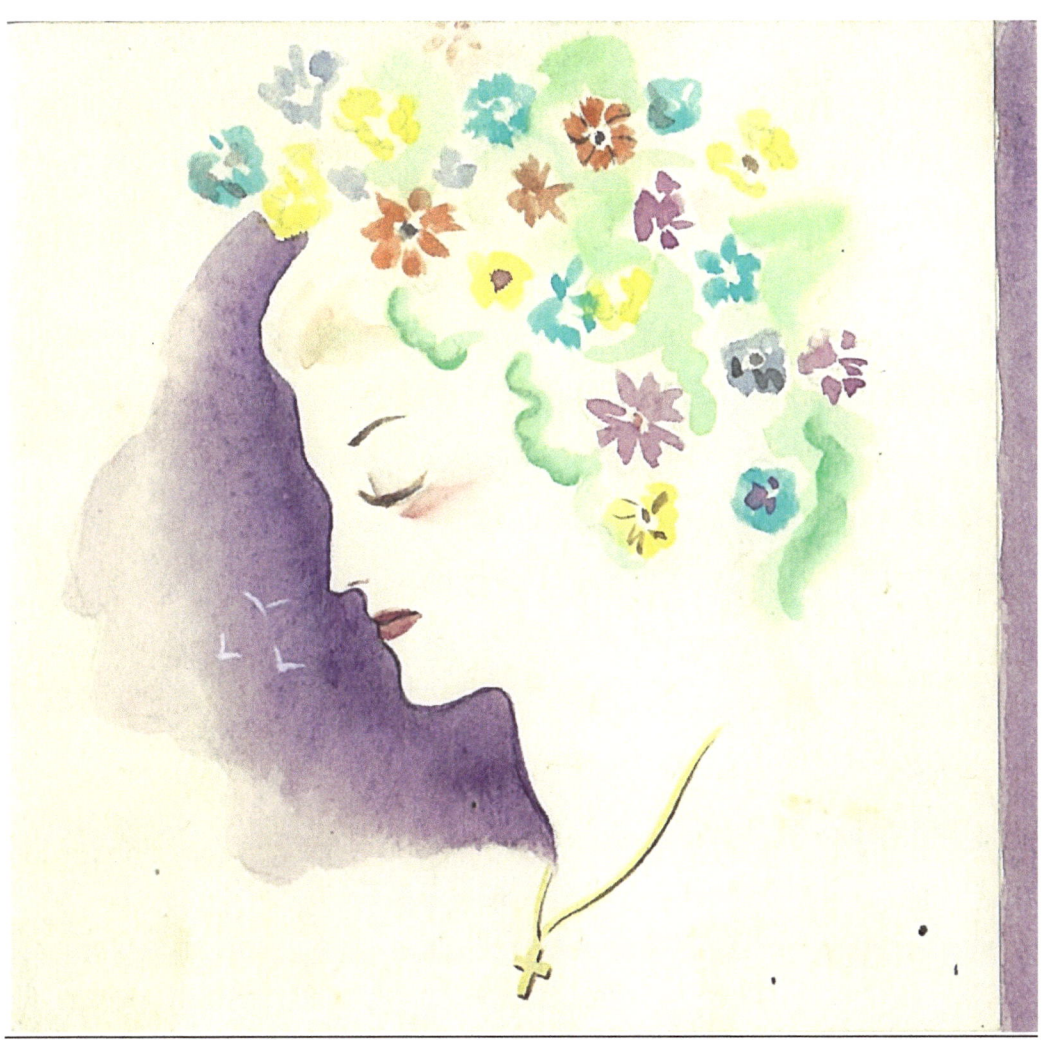

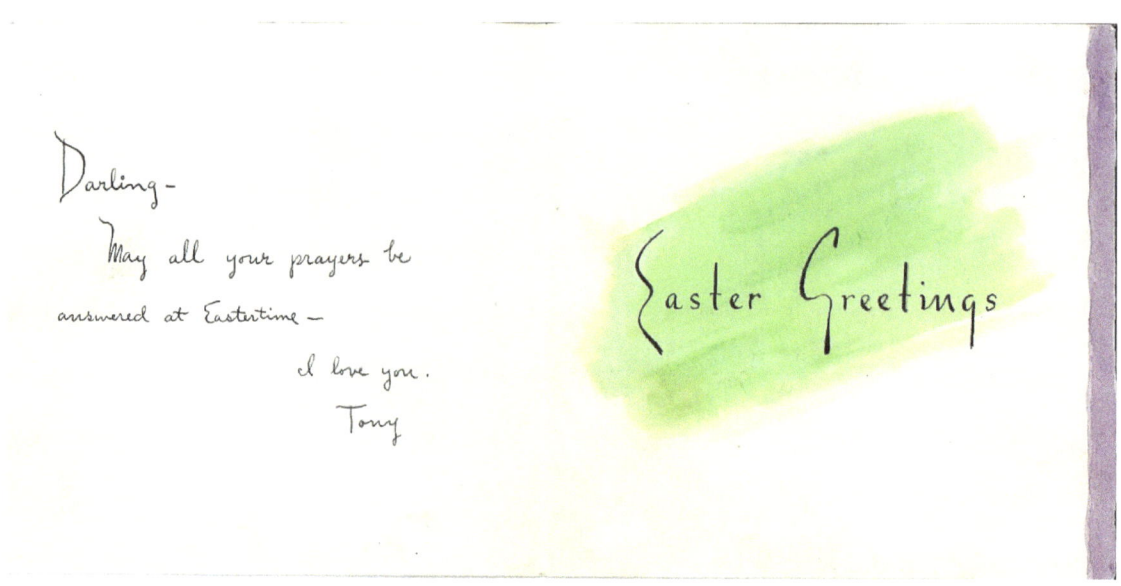

Darling –
    May all your prayers be
answered at Eastertime –
                I love you.
                    Tony

Easter Greetings

HAPPY BIRTHDAY

Mom's Birthday is May 28th, 1920. This is her first Birthday Card from Dad that we have.

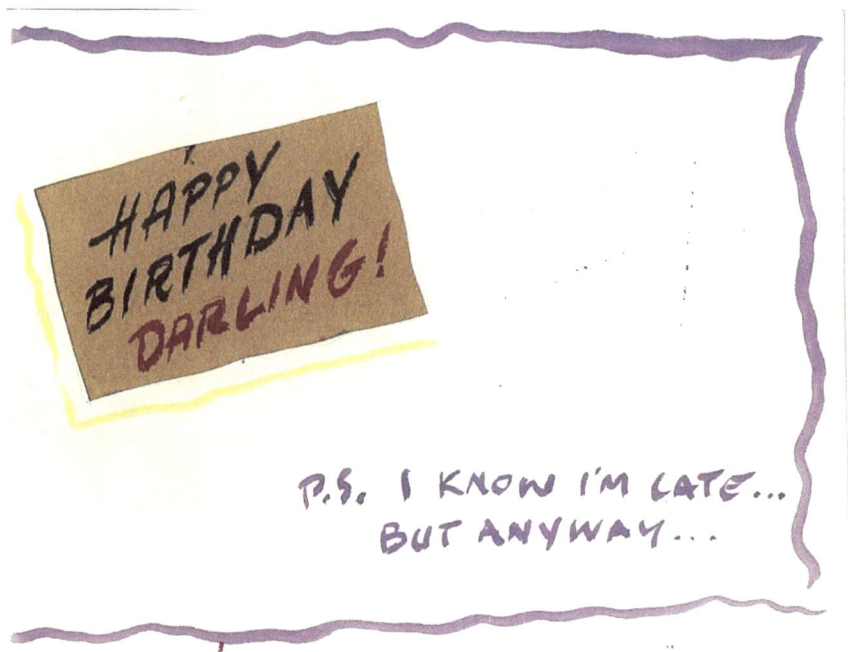

HAPPY BIRTHDAY DARLING!

P.S. I KNOW I'M LATE...
BUT ANYWAY...

The above front flap features a cutout showing " **HAPPY BIRTHDAY DARLING!**"

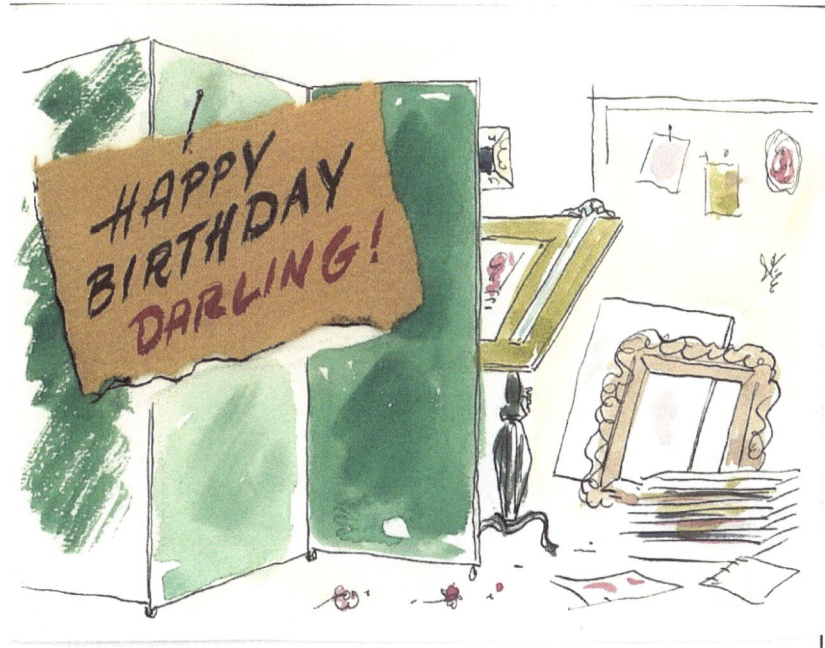

The inside shows a studio in which Dad has obviously been very busy. Dad was studying art at the time. I absolutely recognize the ornate drawing table pedestal and T-Square. I grew up with those pieces in Dad's art area in the basement.

My only other comment about this card is its lack of timing. If I were around at the time, I would have said, "Come on Dad. Get on the ball!" But as they say... "Better Late Than Never."

SECOND CHRISTMAS CARD

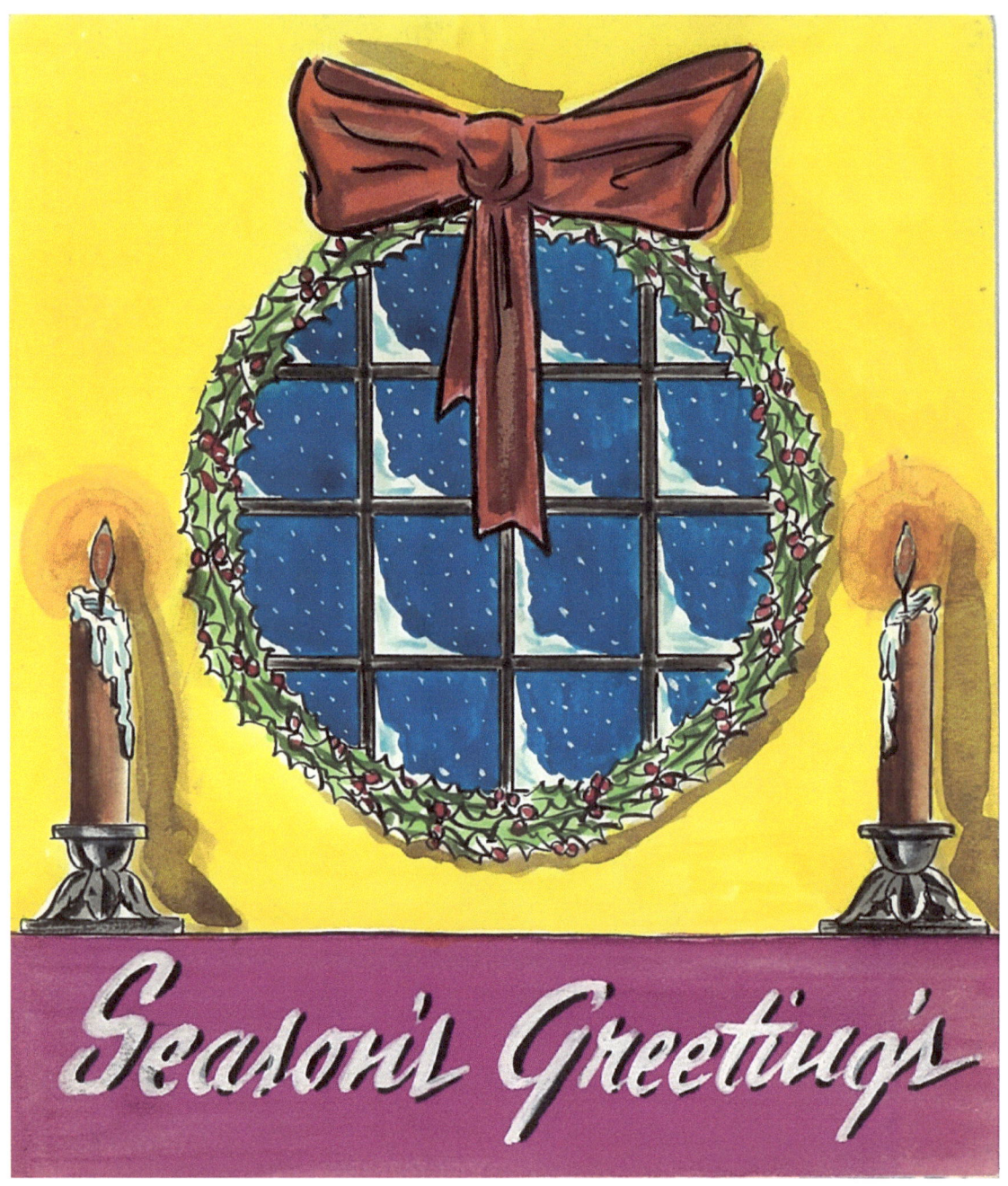

It's such a nice front cover to this card. Even the wax on the candles burns to frame the window so nicely.

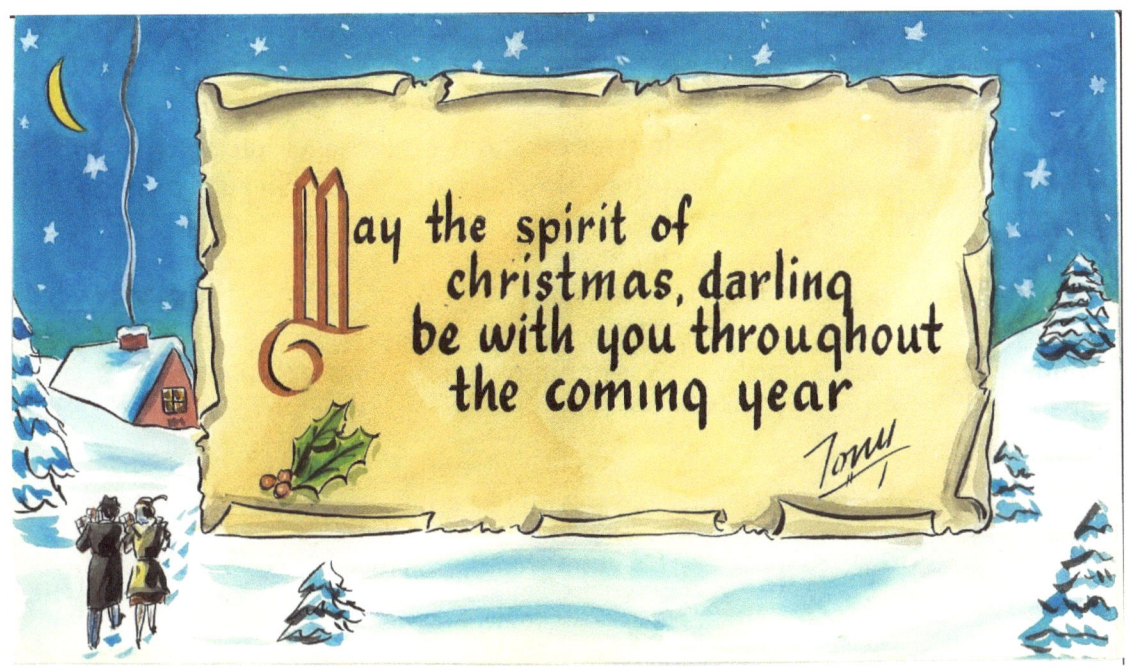

The card opens to a beautiful idyllic and bucolic scene. The perfect "White Christmas" that Bing Crosby sings about. (Dad loved Bing Crosby, second only to Frank Sinatra.)

However, events abroad were anything but idyllic and bucolic. Hitler had just invaded Poland in the action that is generally considered the beginning of World War II.

MOM AND DAD'S ENGAGEMENT

I want to believe that Dad asked Mom for her hand in marriage exactly as it is drawn on the front of this Birthday Card. And I have little reason to believe otherwise. But other than barbequing, I don't remember Dad cooking anything (let alone baking cakes). However, as I am now beginning to realize, Dad as a younger man would have constantly surprised me.

Incidentally, this card's artistic sytle is definitely more representative of Dad's signature style for the next number of years.

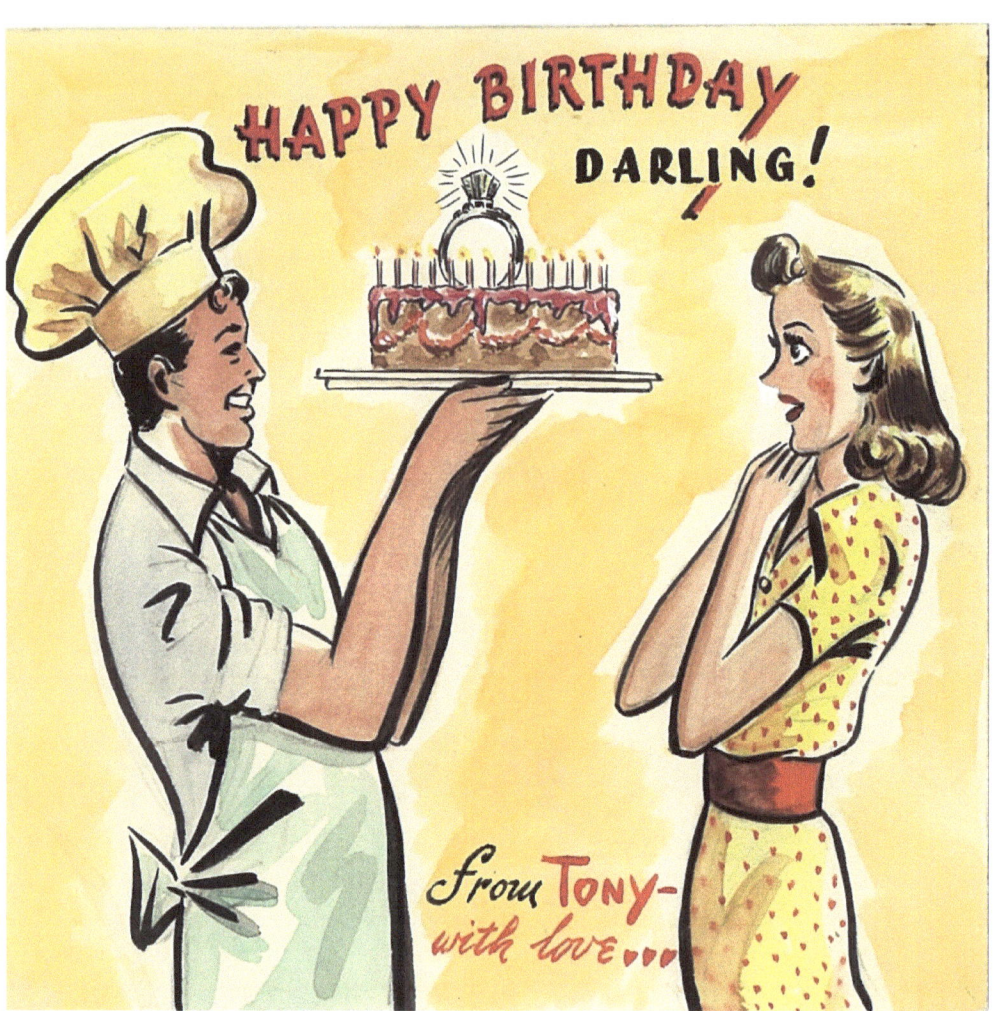

HAPPY EASTER SWEETHEART

This card below is dated exactly three years after their high school prom. Mom is wearing the same dress she was wearing in the previous Engaement/Birthday Card, though she did change her belt. (Ha!)

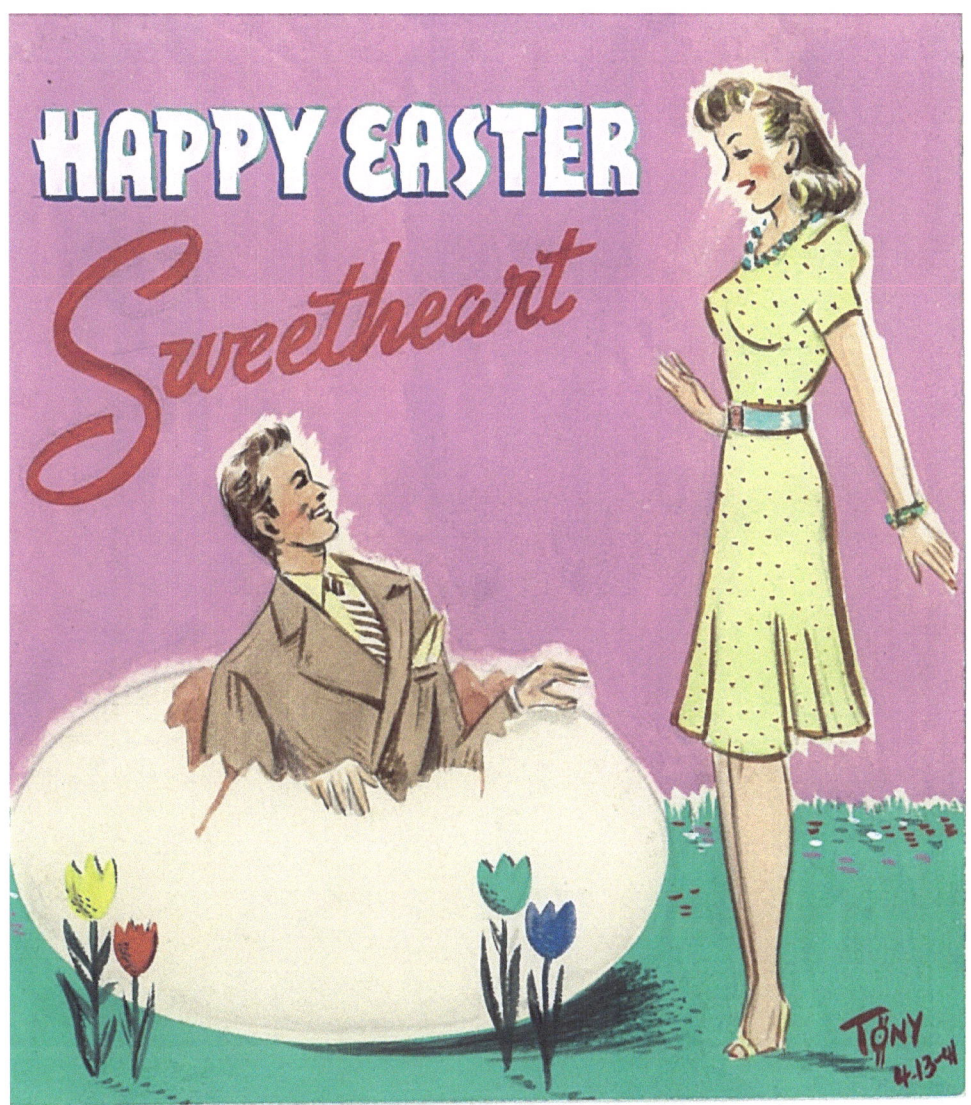

While Dad was surprising Mom by breaking out of a giant Easter Egg, World War II was well underway.

According to Dad's military records, he enlisted in the army later that year in September 1941. The exact reasons for his enlistment are still unknown to me. Of course, when Japan attacked Pearl Harbor three months after Dad joined the army, on December 7th, the U.S. abandoned its isolationism policy and entered the war. So, Dad certainly would have been drafted soon afterwards.

DAD AND OTHER QUEENS TRAINEES SHIFTED TO SOUTH

As a trainee in the Army, this article from a local newspaper lists Dad as one of the Queens natives being transferred from close-by Fort Dix in New Jersey to Fort Bragg, North Carolina.

QUEENS TRAINEES SHIFTED TO SOUTH

A large group of North Queens trainees, recently inducted into the Army at Fort Dix, N. J., has been transferred to the field artillery replacement training center at Fort Bragg, N. C. They are:

LONG ISLAND CITY: Henry F. McImerney, James R. Burns, Carl P. Deroti.

ASTORIA: Albert M. Mayer, Joseph DiGianno, Anthony W. Grande.

CORONA: Frank J. D'Emarese, Frank J. Erato, George A. Heerdt.

ELMHURST: Roy G. Rummel.

JACKSON HEIGHTS: Alfred H. Meese.

MASPETH: Simon Schockett.

Private Salvatore P. Cosmo of 29-06 200th street, Bayside West, has been promoted to sergeant. Sergeant Cosmo, an electrician in civilian life, enlisted March 22, 1939, and for two years was stationed in the Canal Zone. Last July he was transferred to the quartermaster replacement center at Camp Lee, Va.

DAD'S FIRST CHRISTMAS IN THE ARMY

The first Christmas away from Mom (as a couple) is sent from Fort Brag, North Carolina in late December 1941.

I love that dream-like, far-a-way look in Dad's eyes and how his face is flushed with love.

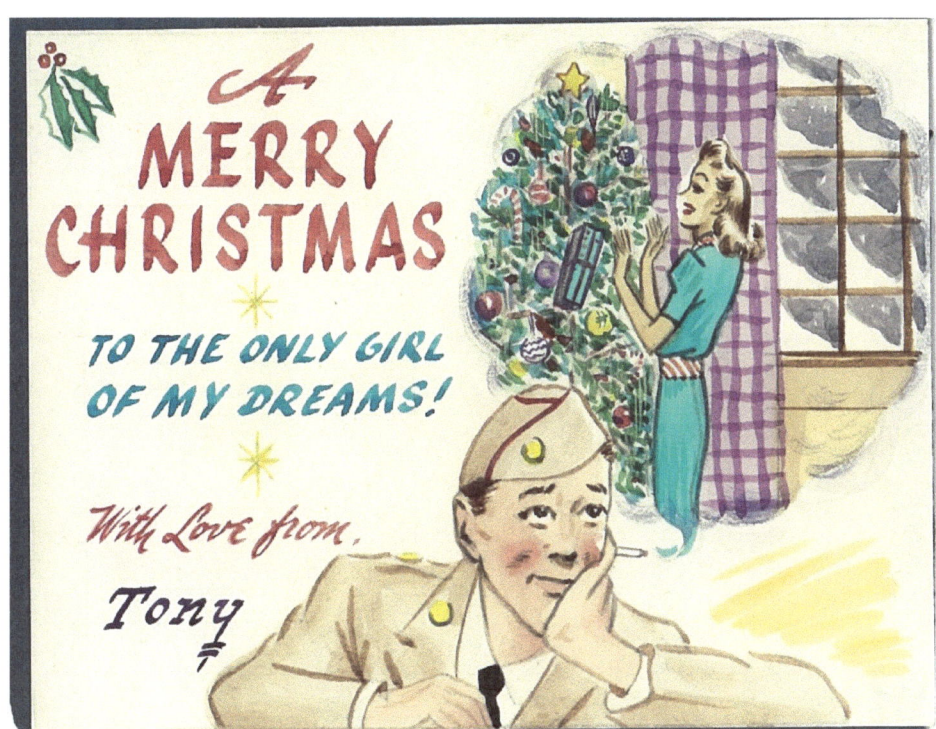

LETTER TO HIS BROTHER JOE

The following month (January 1942), my Dad writes a letter from Fort Bragg to his younger brother, my Uncle Joe in which he talks about, among other things "going to Raleigh and having a "swell time – boy!" as well as the music he has been listening to and how wonderful the climate is there.

But then he gets right to the point and asks my Uncle Joe for a loan. He is asking for a whopping Five Dollars! Laughable now, right?

"I haven't changed," he writes. So, obviously this isn't the first time Dad has asked his younger brother for money. Dad also writes that he is anxious to hear where and when he'll be "shipped out" and that he should hear any day. As it turns out, it is months before he heads overseas, by way of Fort Jackson, also in North Carolina. By the way, Uncle Joe was a musician therefore, the reference to "jive", a popular dance/music style of the 1930's.

Monday, Jan. 26

Dear Joe,

How are you, kid? Is everything alright? How's the jive coming along? Have you seen those pictures yet? I hope you enjoyed them. Saw "Johnny Eager" and that was fine too.

Went to Raleigh and had a swell time - boy! the southern climate is terrific. Sure would like to settle down here some day -

We still don't know where the heck we are going or when! But we'll get the works in a few days - Hope it's soon, I'm getting sick of this fooling around. Hope we go to Dix, ok, but the chances are very slight.

Have you heard anything about Alex! Boy, I'm so anxious to hear about him. Let me know, hu? Heard a few records in Raleigh - Jimmy Lunceford's - "By the River St. Marie" and on the other side "Melancoly Baby" what swell arrangements!

Joe, I'm going to ask you for a favor - to come to the point - I'm broke! You see we were to be paid this week but we may not because of the shipping out business - will well, money goes so fast the few nights you get away that before you know it - bingo, it's gone. I just got through borrowing $5.00 and would like to pay the boy back before we get out. We'll be getting $30 next month and I'll try to sent it back to you - I haven't changed, have I - You can't imagine how it hurts my pride to ask you but I can't tell the people about it cause they gave me $15 during the week of my birthday - Keep it under your hat - Send it to this address - I'll get it if I'm at another join - make it a registered letter.

Well, tonight, I'll play some pool in the recreation hall - and I'll be thinking of those nights we played together - remember? And you always trimmed me, too! But I'm getting better - So long and write soon! Your brother, Tony

THE WEDDING

My guess is once Dad learns he is going to be shipped overseas to the front lines in Africa, he and Mom decide to get married before he leaves. So he heads up north and comes home, marries Mom, has a one-day Honeymoon and afterwards goes off to war. Just like that!

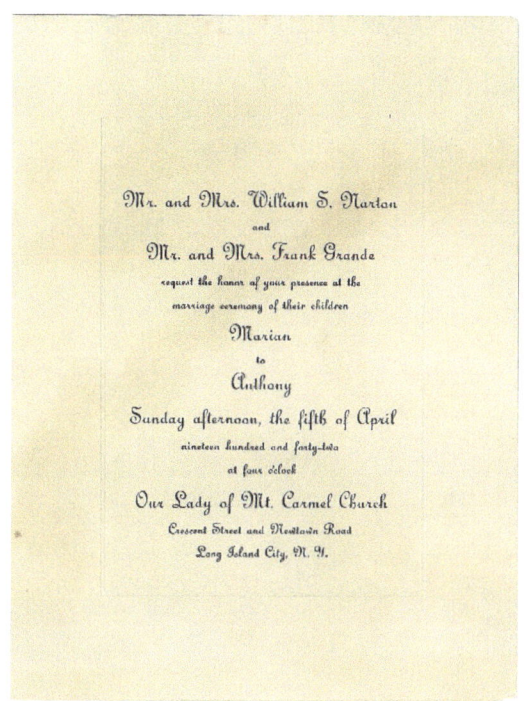
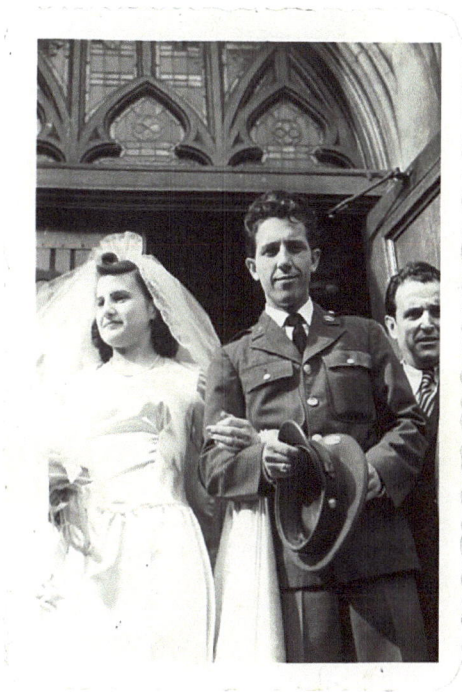

THE HONEYMOON

So, the Honeymoon was short, simple and sweet.   I can't help but think that nevertheless, they were overjoyed with their brief time together as man and wife.

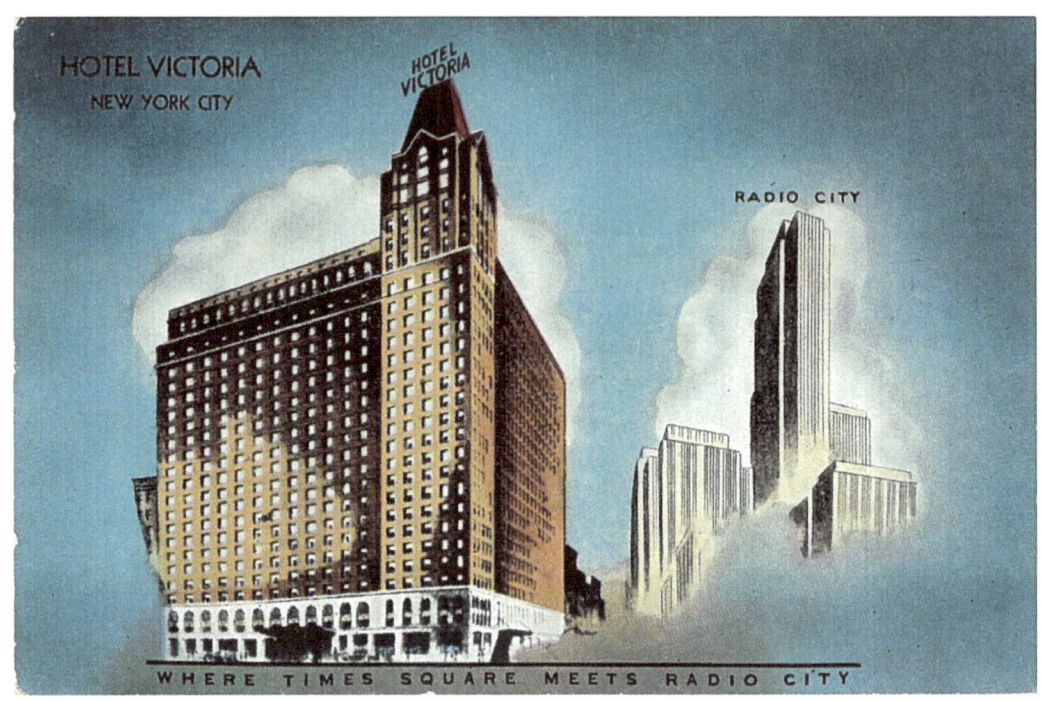

On Google Maps, it appears that this hotel is now an office building. I recognized the façade outside the lower floors as it was partially maintained.

MOM'S FIRST BIRTHDAY CARD AS MRS. GRANDE

Mom is "The Sweetest Wife In The World" on her first Birthday as a married woman. It's approximately two months after their honeymoon. Dad however, is still state-side at Fort Jackson.

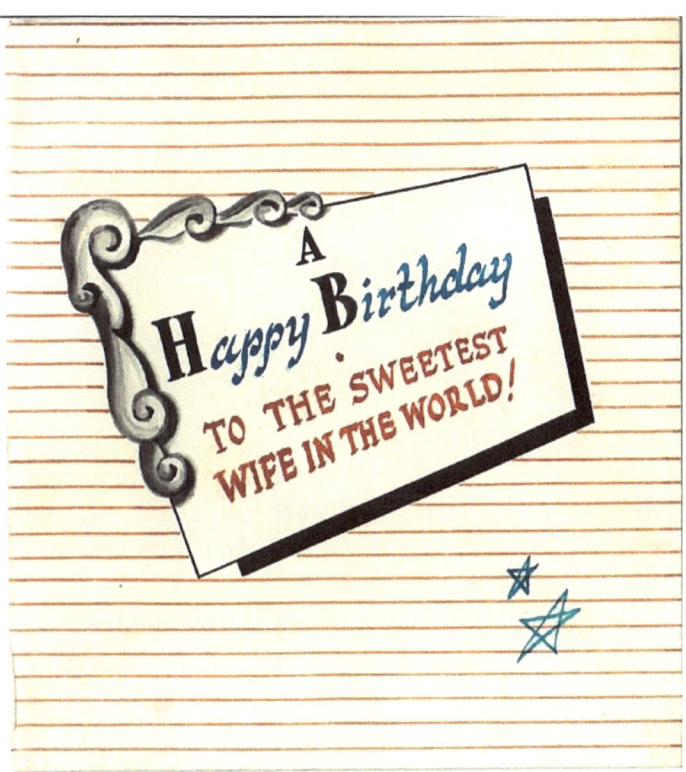

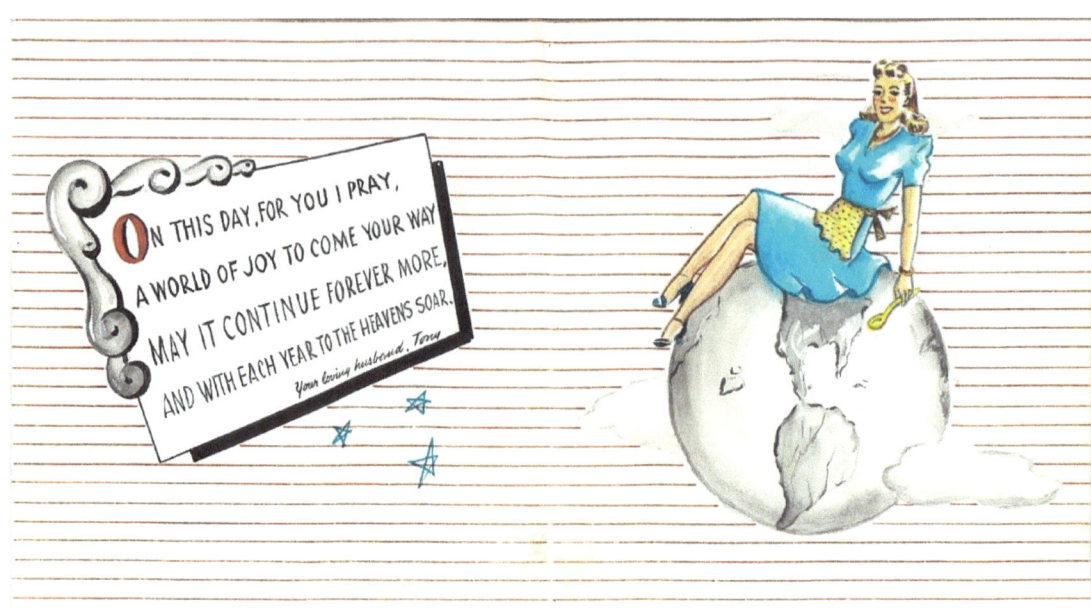

Dad's poetry has improved some, from their "Prom" date, don't you think? The religious references seem odd (again) coming from my Dad. Depicting Mom, domesticated --- in an apron holding a ladel --- is however, definitely our Dad's vision of Mom."

SEASON'S GREETINGS, 1942

We have nothing for the next 7 months until the "Holidays" at the end of 1942. Dad is now stationed in North Africa, as the card's front cover shows. Dad was an army "map maker" by virtue of his steady, artistic hand. Though his work was vital to America's war effort, and he certainly was in harm's way, it was somewhat less heroic than those on the battlefields he drew where many of America's "Greatest Generation" fought and died. Tom Brokaw coined that phrase. It describes that generation perfectly.

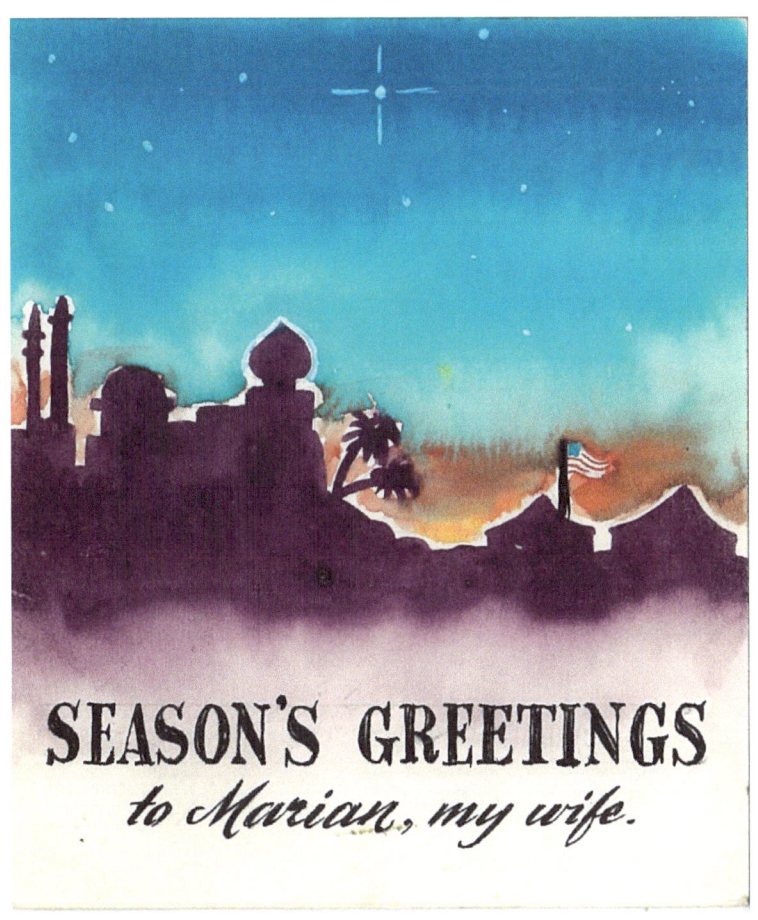

SEASON'S GREETINGS
to Marian, my wife.

Incidentally, Dad would have nightmares about the Army all through his adult life, a stark emotional contrast from the beautiful landscape he drew on this card's cover, complete with the North Star and Old Glory.

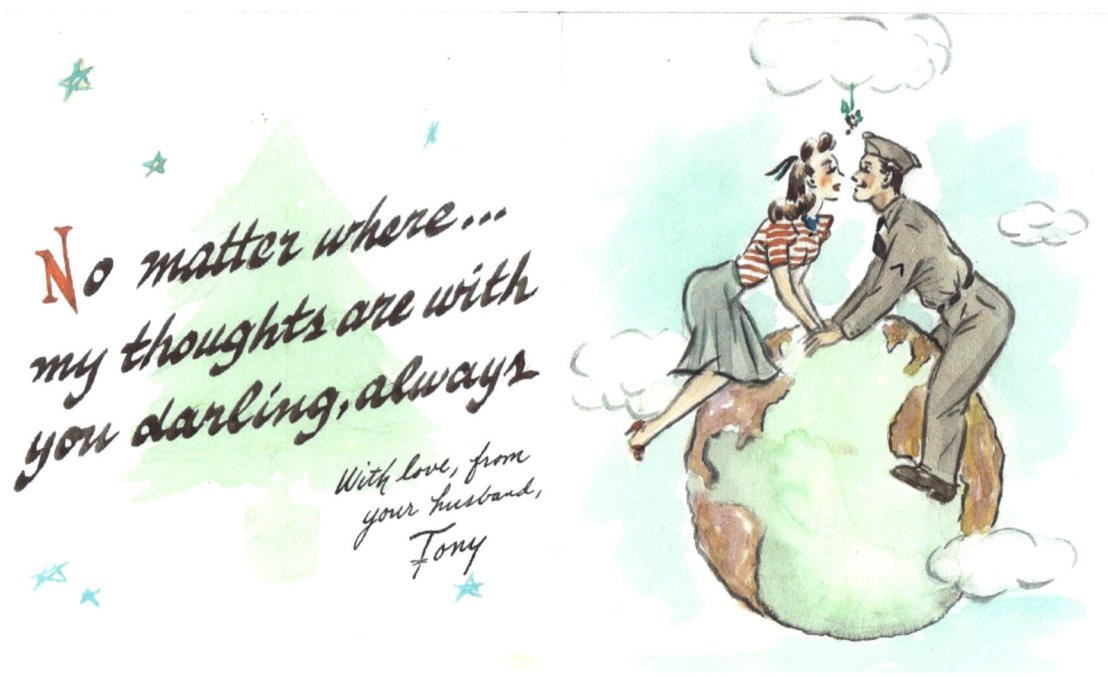

The inside of this card is rendered more in Dad's "cartoon" style of drawing.

As if he needed mistetoe to kiss Mom! I love how he places himself in Africa and Mom in the good old US of A!

Dad writes a note on the back of the card:

Dec. 14, 1942

Marian dear,

Well, I _did_ get the time to make you a Christmas card. I just couldn't let you down. Hope you like it.

With love,

Tony

P.S. Mail follows.

I can picture Mom now and how she would have loved to receive these card and letters from Dad. I can see her excitedly opening the envelope, reading the card and sharing it with her family and friends. (Now I'm missing her terribly.)

SEASON'S GREETINGS AND PARTY INVITATION

For his Commanding Officer, Dad creates this Holiday Invitation in 1942 for his army company, The 66th Engineer Topographic Company. Their mission was to provide maps of the surrounding areas for the fighting effort.

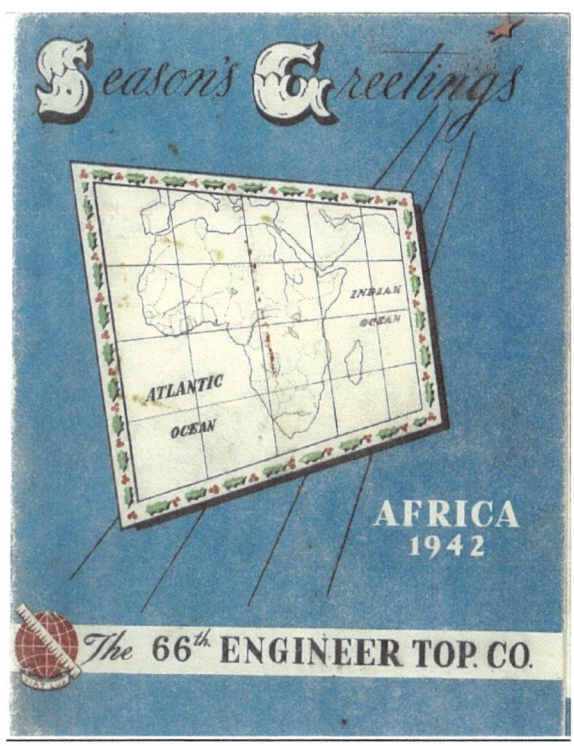 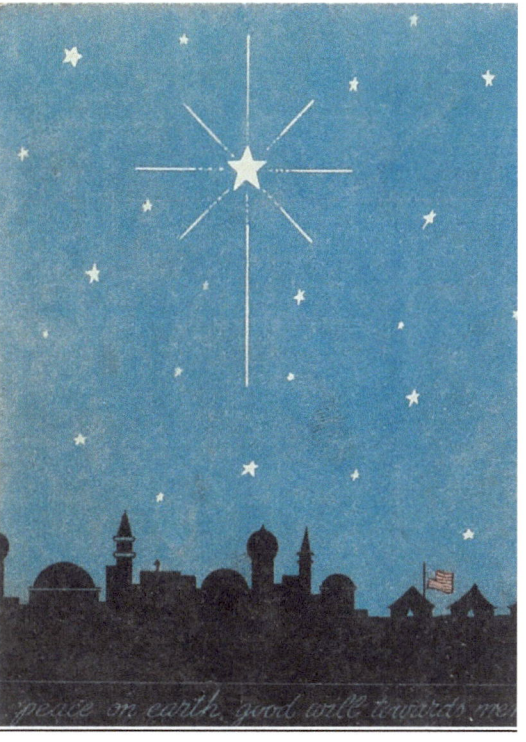

Incidentally, Mom's Holiday Card and this Season's Greetings Card share a similar scene (on the right). Hey, my Dad was very resourceful. Why reinvent the wheel?

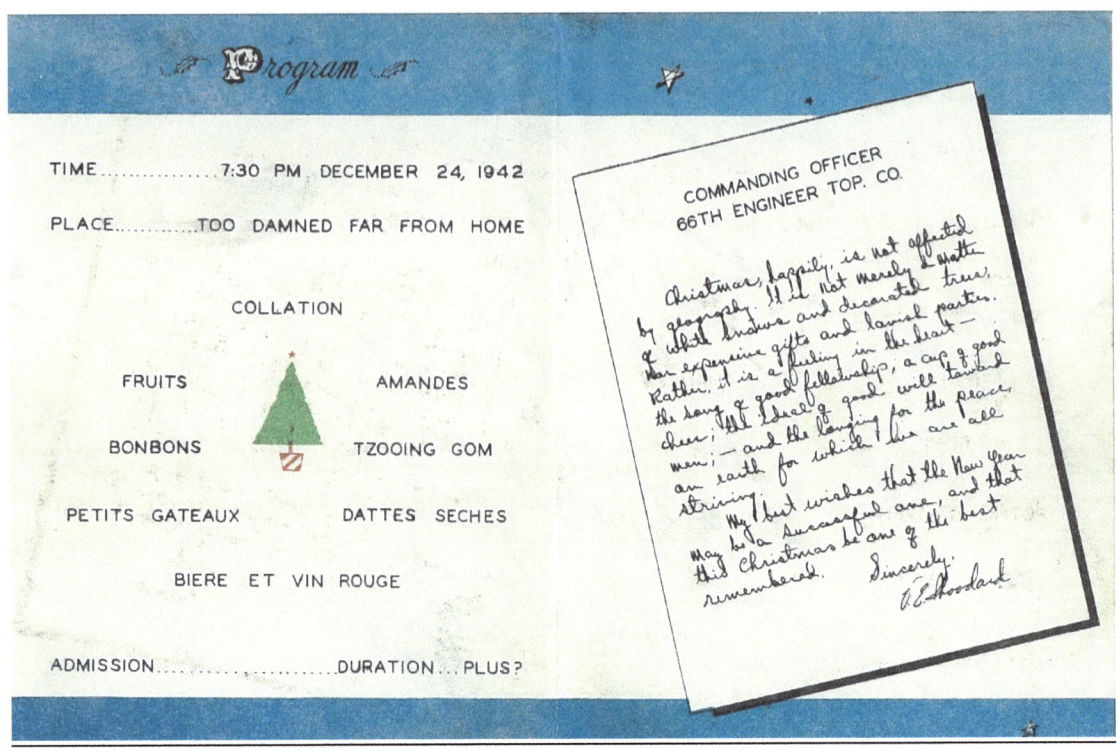

The party menu, which is written in French (they were stationed in Algeria-French Morocco) features snacks, candy, small cakes, almonds, dried dates, beer and red wine. I don't know what "tzooing gom" is! Could it be chewing gum? On a party menu? No, can't be. Can it?

I love the "place" for the party... too damn far from home!

Dad writes a note to Mom on the back of the invitation...

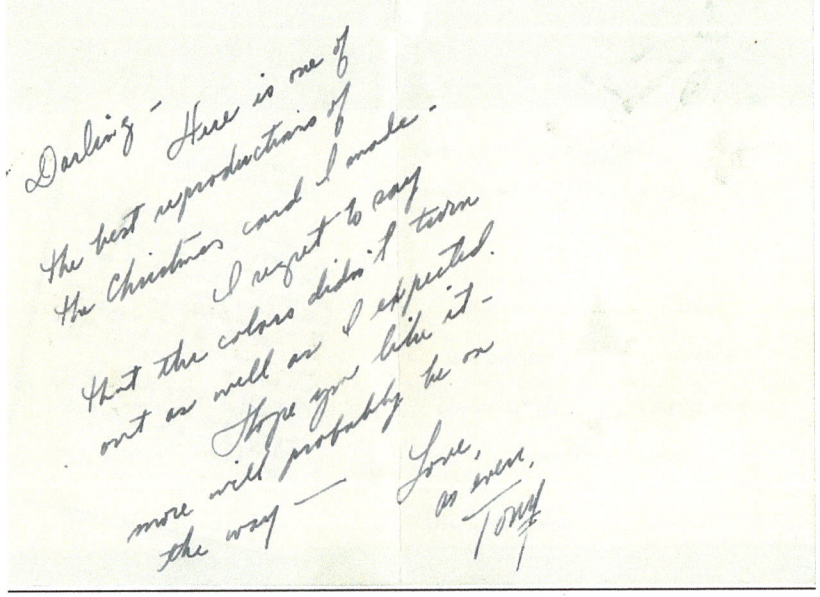

ADDITIONAL INFORMATION ON THE 66TH ENGINEER COMPANY

Lineage and Honors Information (as of 2 October 2012)

66TH ENGINEER COMPANY

Constituted 1 July 1940 in the Regular Army as the 66th Engineer Company

Activated 8 July 1941 at Fort Jackson, South Carolina

Re-designated 1 April 1942 as the 66th Engineer Topographic Company, Corps

Inactivated 30 September 1946 in Japan

Activated 30 November 1946 in Germany

Inactivated 20 June 1948 in Germany

Activated 15 December 1950 at Fort George G. Meade, Maryland

Reorganized and re-designated 1 October 1953 as the 66th Engineer Company

Inactivated 20 March 1972 in Vietnam

Activated 21 December 1976 at Fort Hood, Texas

Inactivated 15 June 1987 at Fort Hood, Texas

Activated 16 October 2005 at Schofield Barracks, Hawaii

CAMPAIGN PARTICIPATION CREDIT

World War II
Algeria-French Morocco
(with arrowhead)
Sicily (with arrowhead)
Naples-Foggia
Rome-Arno
North Apennines
Po Valley
Asiatic-Pacific Theater,
Streamer without inscription

Vietnam
Counteroffensive, Phase II
Counteroffensive, Phase III
Tet Counteroffensive
Counteroffensive, Phase IV
Counteroffensive, Phase V
Counteroffensive, Phase VI
Tet 69/Counteroffensive
Summer-Fall 1969
Winter-Spring 1970
Counteroffensive

Counteroffensive, Phase VII
Consolidation I
Consolidation II

War on Terrorism
Campaigns to be determined

DECORATIONS

Meritorious Unit Commendation (Army), Streamer embroidered ITALY 1944
Meritorious Unit Commendation (Army), Streamer embroidered VIETNAM 1966-1967
Meritorious Unit Commendation (Army), Streamer embroidered VIETNAM 1968
Meritorious Unit Commendation (Army), Streamer embroidered IRAQ 2007-2009
Republic of Vietnam Civil Action Honor Medal, First Class, Streamer embroidered VIETNAM 1967-1970

BY ORDER OF THE SECRETARY OF THE ARMY:

ROBERT J. DALESSANDRO, Director, Center of Military History

MY UNCLE JOE -THE SWELLEST BROTHER

By February 1943, my Uncle Joe is also part of the war effort. He is "The SWELLEST Brother A Guy Could Have In The Service." Since I grew up in the 1960's, I probably would have written, " The GROOVIEST Brother A Guy Could Have In The Service." That sounds equally ridiculous now so I won't make fun of the term, "SWELLEST."

This card and the earlier letter to my Uncle Joe represent the only other record of correspondence we have from my Dad to someone other than my Mom during the war. (Dad also had a sister and another younger brother.) Though we know he did write to his Father and Mother as well.

As you will see inside the card, Hitler and Hirohito take it on the chin. Mussolini is already down on the ground and knocked out.

Incidentally, we only have this black and white photocopy of the card. I was unable to locate the original.

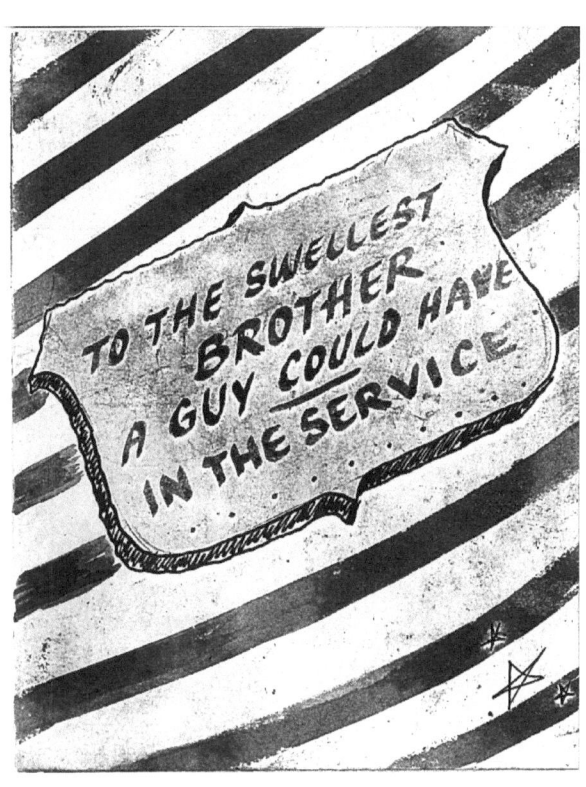

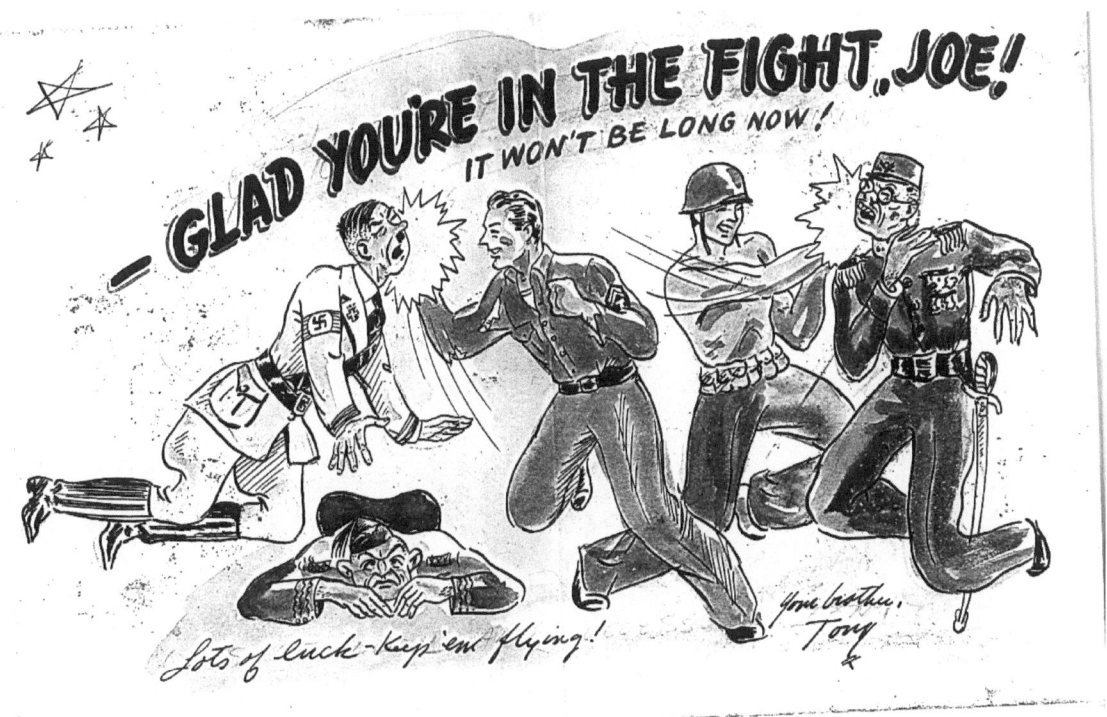

My Uncle Joe was in the Air Force, stationed in London where he loaded bombs onto planes. Therefore, the phrase "Keep 'em flying." He was also the bandleader and saxophone player for the 390th Bombcats Band.

Despite the tradegy my Uncle suffered in his lifetime --- he lost his only son in the Vietnam War and his wife, my Aunt Helene at a young age --- through the years he kept his cool and composure, at least in public. I can't imagine what his private moments were like back then. Now deceased, he is survived by his daughter.

GEE I MISS YOU

This card was sent to my Mom (again from Africa) sometime in early 1943. By this time, Mussolini and Italy had surrendered to the Allies.

One of my Dad's favorite jokes was, "What's the smallest book in the world?"
Answer: "Italian war heroes." The joke must have started right after the surrender.
Sometimes he would add to the end of the joke, "Italians are lovers, not fighters".

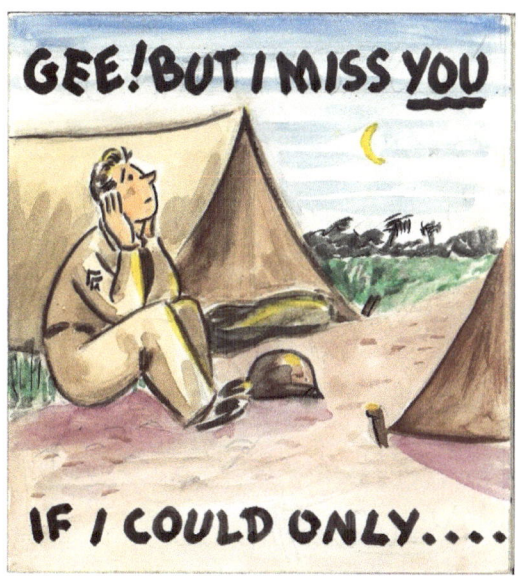 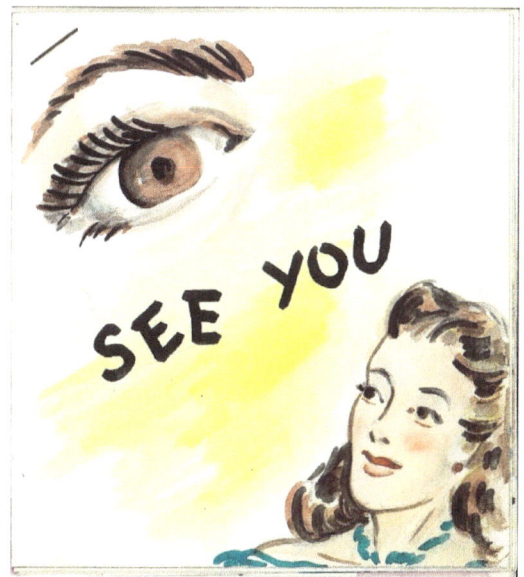

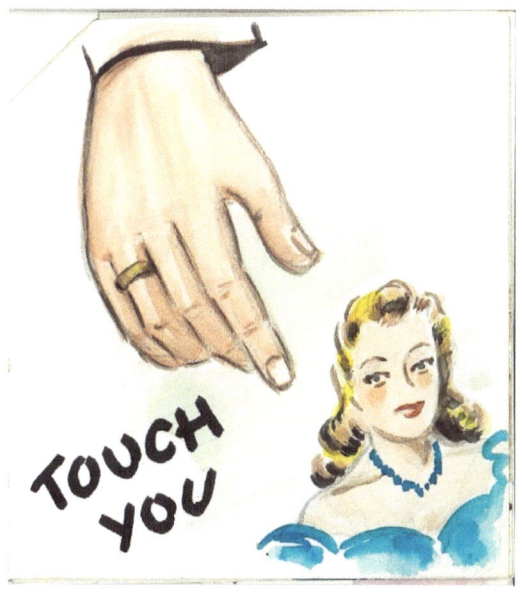 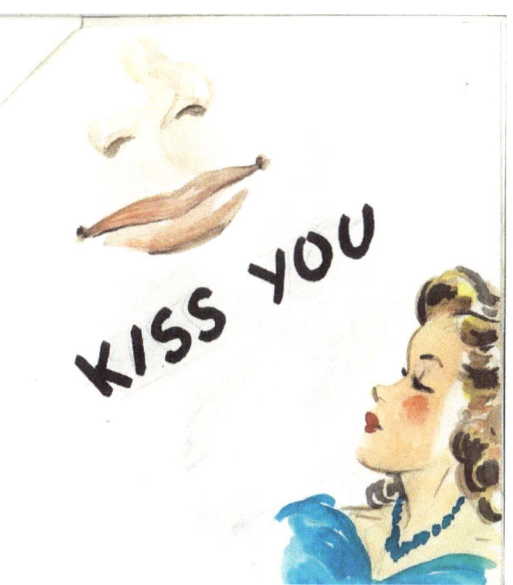

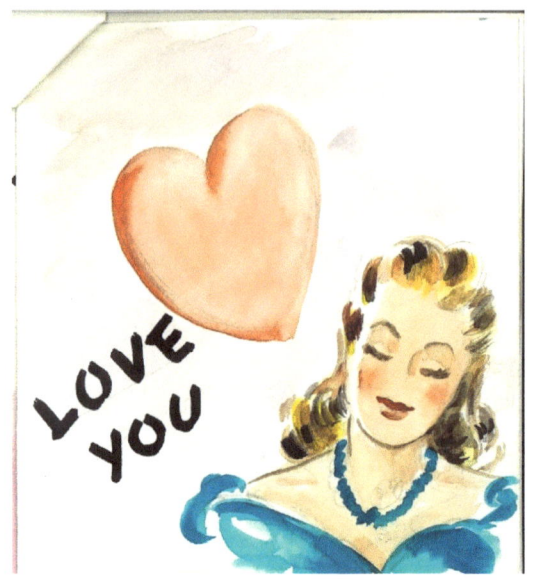
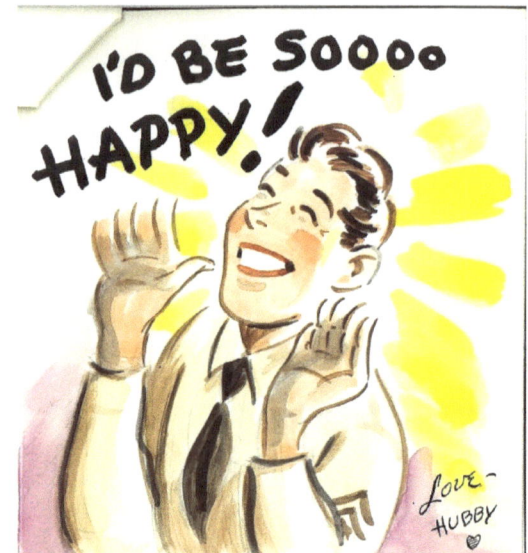

Certainly this isn't one of his most artisitic cards but I love the pure emotion and love it conveys, especially at the end.

THEIR FIRST ANNIVERSARY

Each of the Anniversary Cards, beginning with the first one below was always created with a little extra effort and time. Also, Dad repeatedly used a thicker card stock.

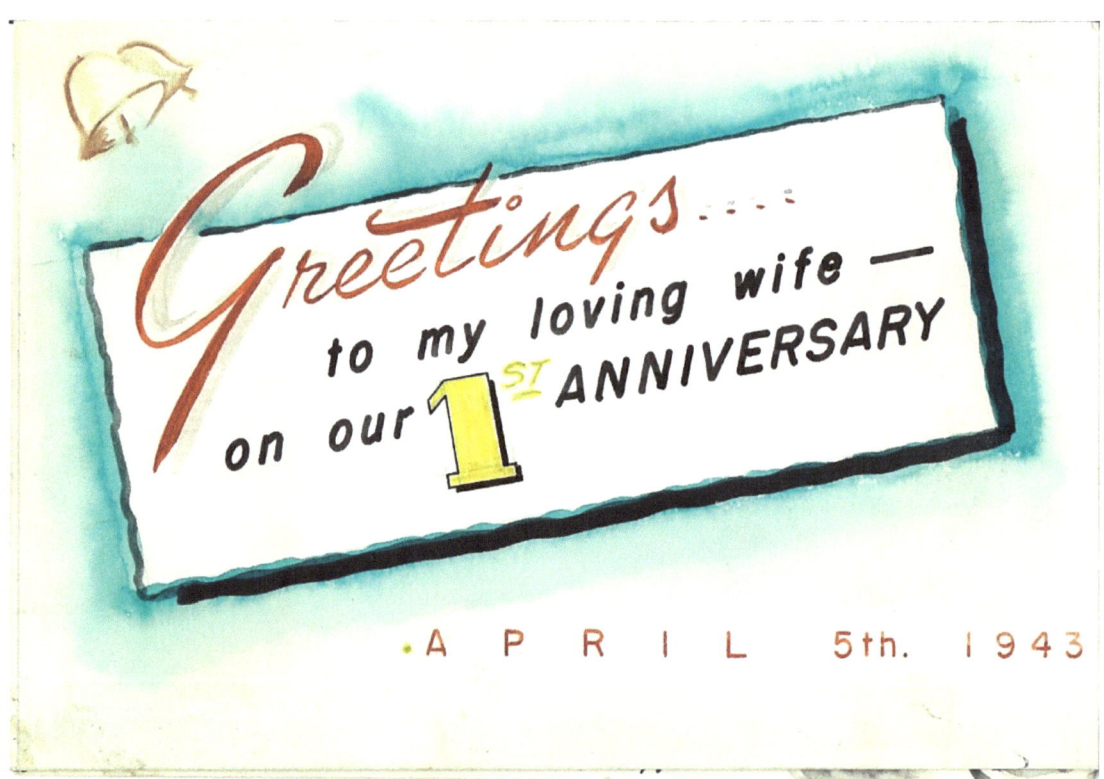

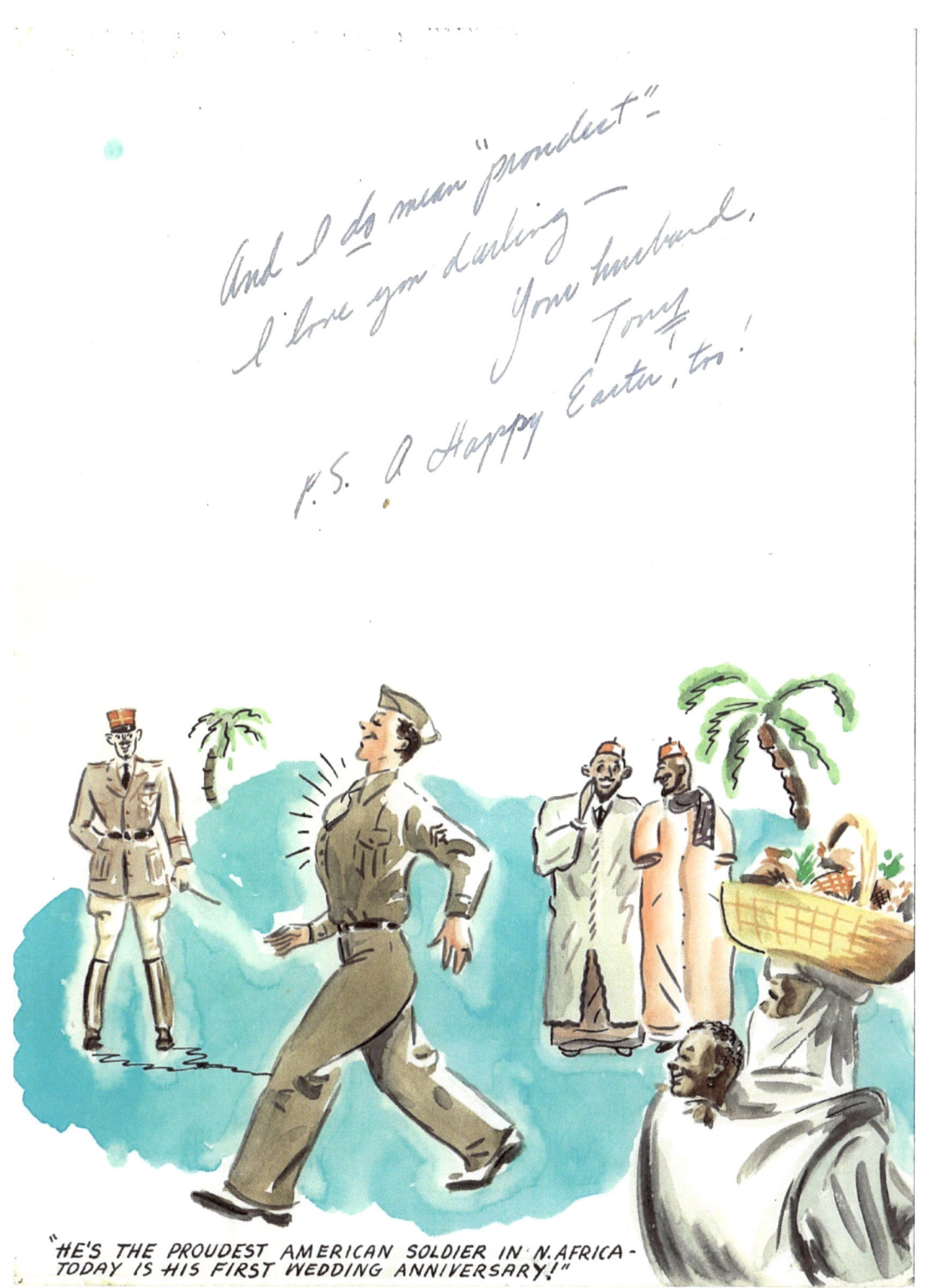

And I *do* mean "proudest" —
I love you darling —
Your husband,
Tony
P.S. A Happy Easter, too!

"HE'S THE PROUDEST AMERICAN SOLDIER IN N. AFRICA - TODAY IS HIS FIRST WEDDING ANNIVERSARY!"

If ever there was a drawing of a man wearing his pride on his sleeve (or in this case on his chest) this one certainly would be it... in spades! Dad was a very proud man indeed!

I'm sure the experience of being stationed in North Africa wasn't as "friendly" as this cartoon of him walking around North Africa represents. As smarter people than I probably know, the North African Campaign was fought between the Allies and Axis Powers due to their colonial interests in Africa dating from the late 19th century.

V-MAIL

Dated only a day after the First Anniversary Card, Dad's Easter Card is drawn on a "V-Mail Letter".

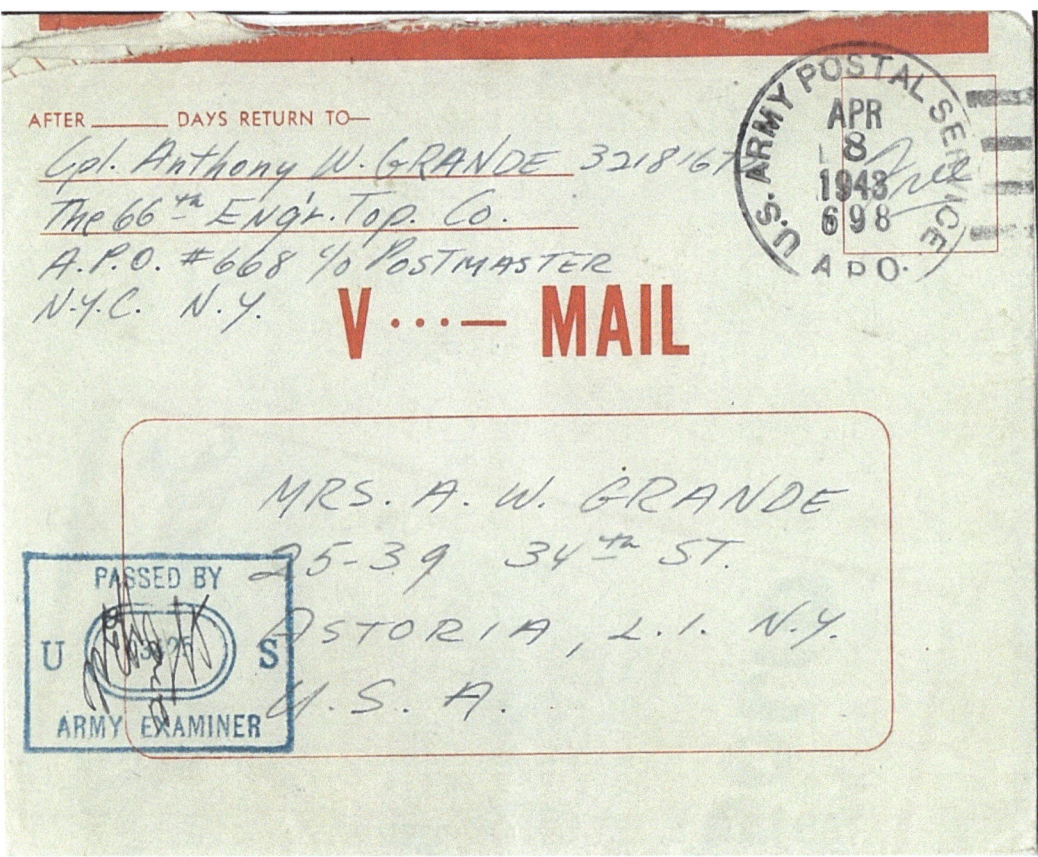

It unfolds to show…

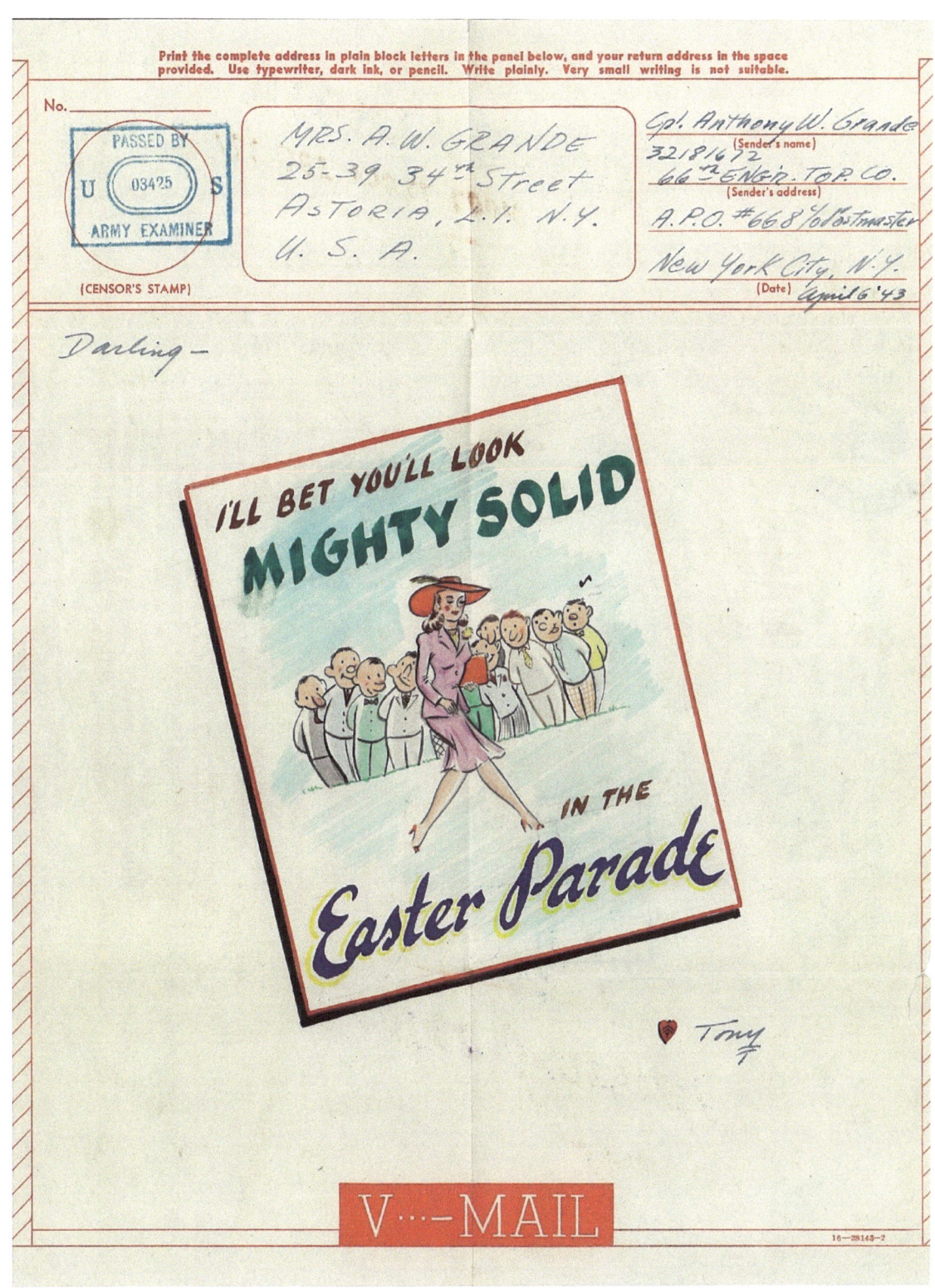

As you can see, Dad draws Mom in the Easter Parade looking "MIGHTY SOLID," apparently an expression of praise in those days. Men are admiring her, while at least one is whistling, though quite innocently. Even now, I still laugh sometimes when I see this drawing.

Notice the address on the V-mail. Along with Mom's parents, she lived at 25-39 34st Street in Astoria which became the home in which my Mom and Dad raised my brothers and me. By the way, Mom's three brothers were also in the military during World War II. Everyone came home. The odds must have been more than mildly against that very fortunate ending.

MOM'S 23RD BIRTHDAY- SECOND BIRTHDAY WITH DAD AT WAR

This is the second birthday of Mom's while Dad was away. He draws himself watching Mom blow out the candles on her cake "in spirit." Only after a number of views did I realize that Dad drew himself "in spirit." I also just realized that Dad drew 23 candles! Perfect!

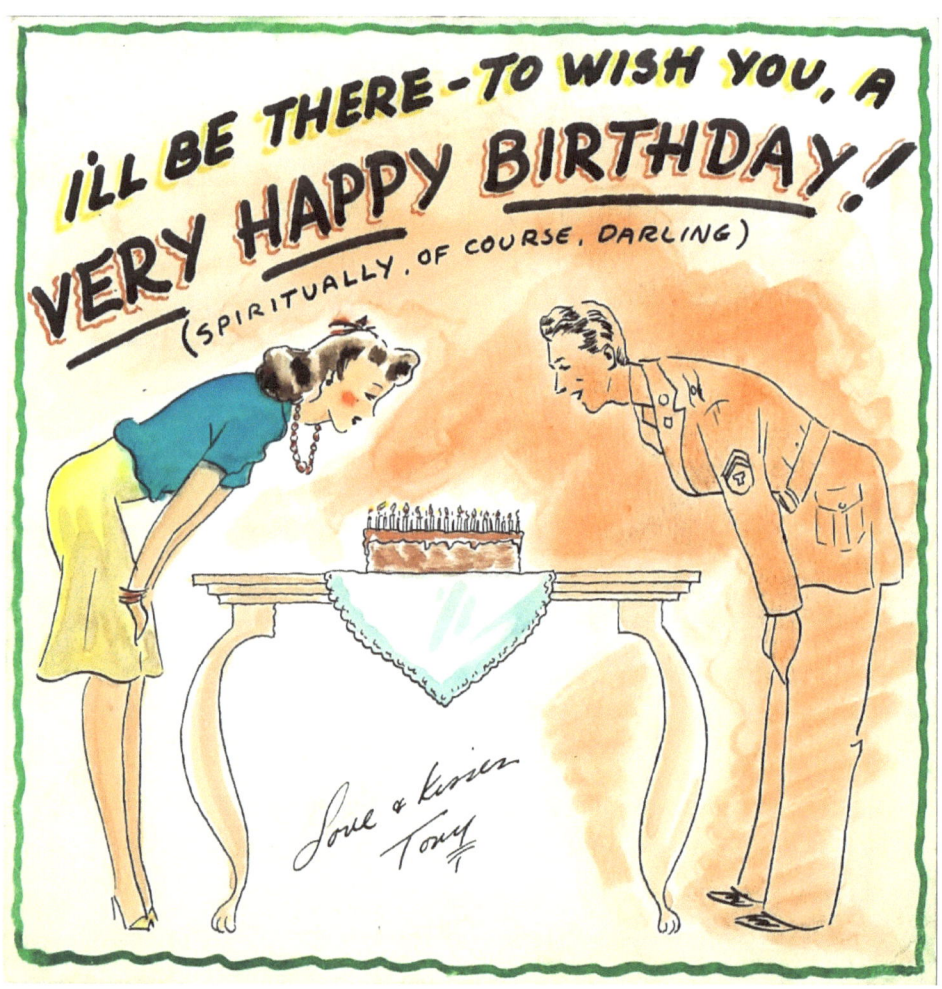

NEED AN OCCASION?

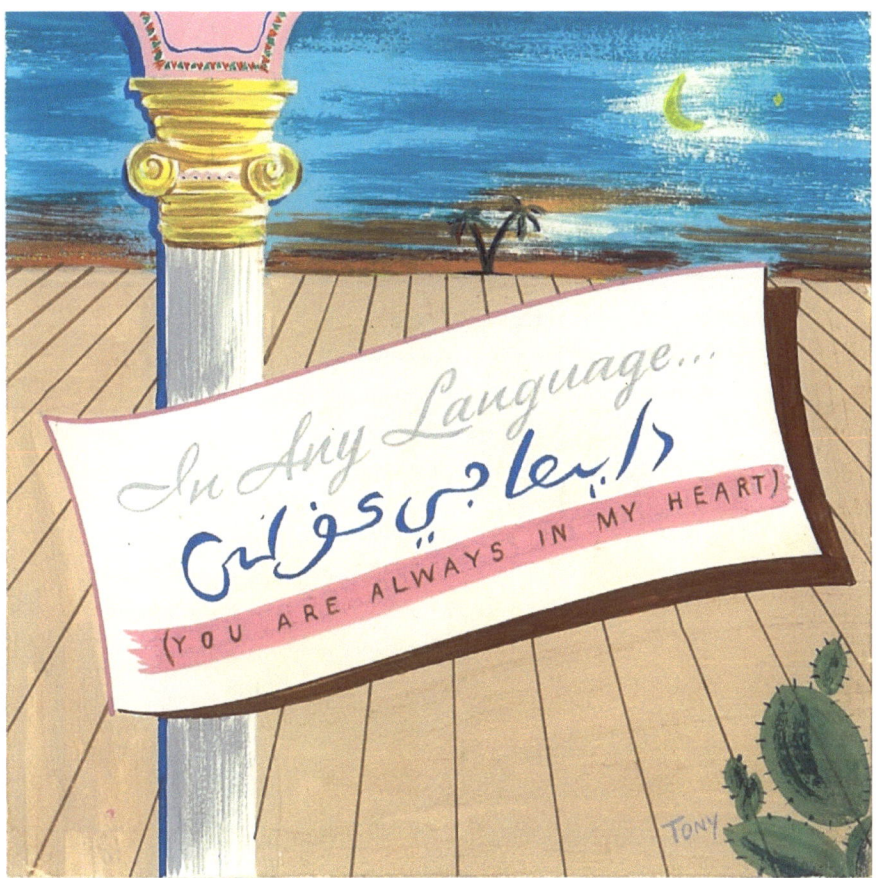

There's no reason for this card other than for my Dad to write Mom that he loves her and that she is always in his heart. (What better reason to send a card?)

Dad writes on the back of the card... *Just like that – "I Love You"*

Your husband Tony

August 9, 1943

This card obviously continues to reflect his time in the North Africa Campaign, which according to the history books ended in May of 1943. So, the campaign here ended three months before this card was sent. That means either Dad's company stayed behind after the fighting ceased (this seems unlikely though) or he sent this card from his next base sometime after he created it in North Africa. Dad and his company's next stop was Italy (his country of birth) where they joined the invasion as reflected in the next card.

SEASONS GREETINGS 1943

This is the cover. Beautiful, don't you agree?

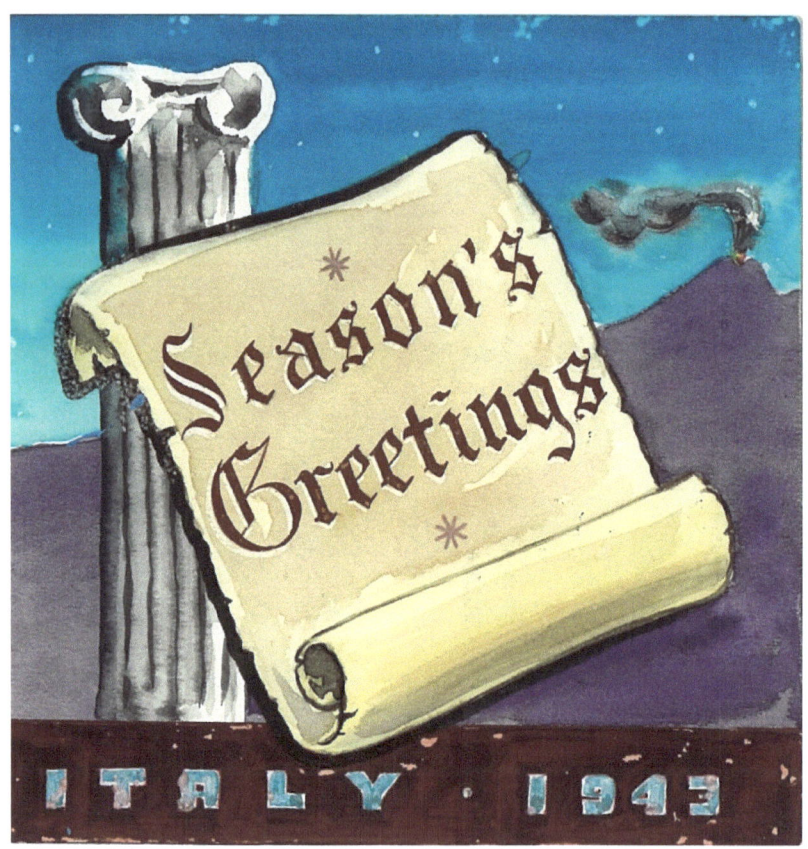

Notice the active volcano in the background. From what I've read, the volcano would either be Mount Etna, Mount Stromboli (which has been on low boil for a while) or perhaps Mount Vesuvius, which last erupted, coincidentally (or not) around 1943.

I like to think it is Mount Stromboli, which happens to be the active volcano (and only active volcano I've ever seen live) that I glimpsed one night while on a Mediterranean Cruise. The captain woke us all up in the middle of the night to see it. Perpetual fireworks. It was well worth losing a little sleep.

A SECOND 1943 HOLIDAY CARD

Here's where some confusion exists. In piecing the cards together chronologically, this next card also falls into the 1943 Holiday Season timeframe. Let's suffice to say Dad had some extra spare time and felt especially loving of Mom this Holiday Season. This is the cover of the card followed by the inside and back.

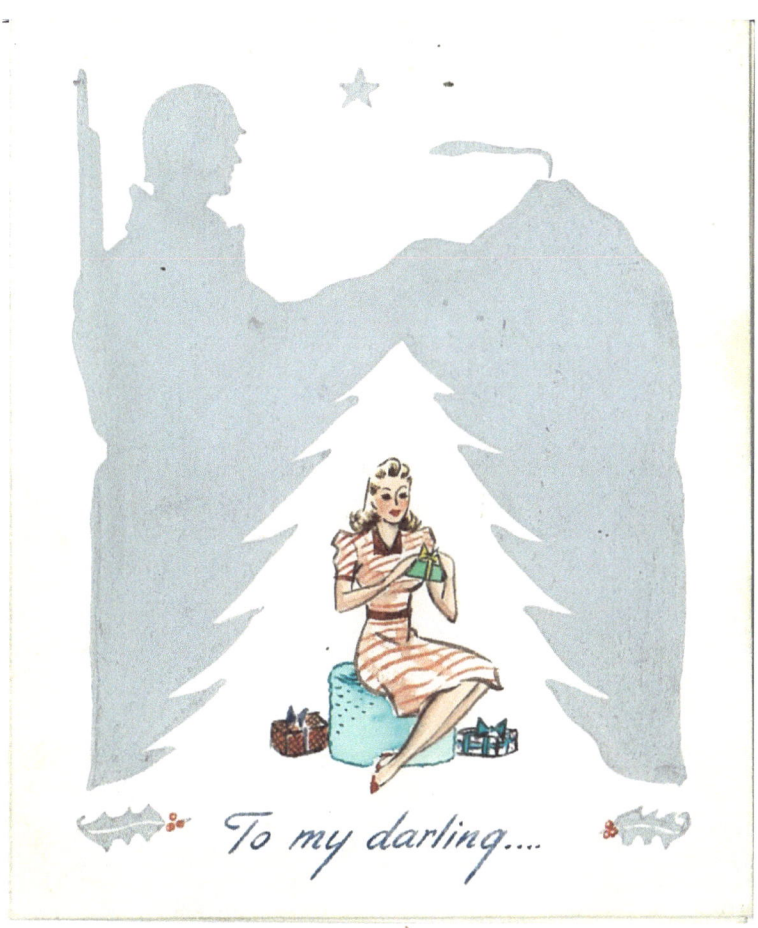

To my darling....

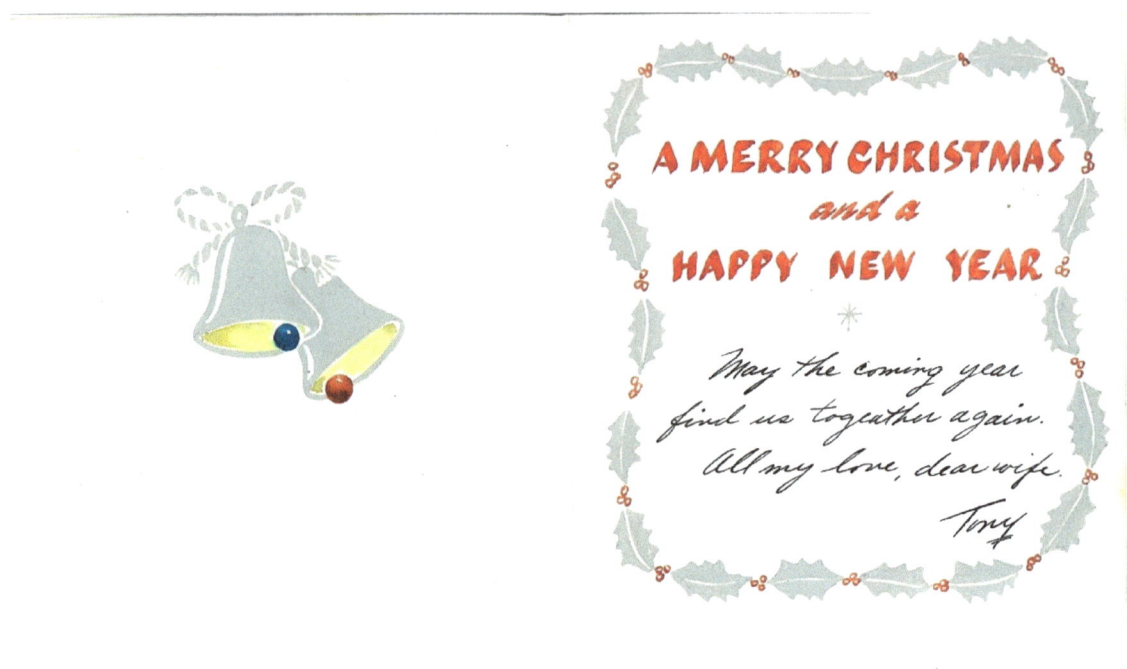

A MERRY CHRISTMAS
and a
HAPPY NEW YEAR

May the coming year
find us together again.
All my love, dear wife.
Tony

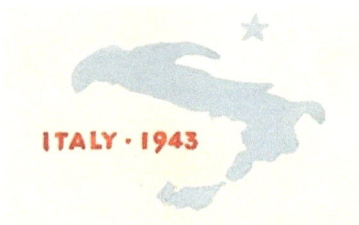

ITALY · 1943

There's Italy with the familiar North Star (we've seen it a number of times now) as it appeared on the back of the card.

MOM AND DAD'S SECOND ANNIVERSARY

There's quite a different theme to the Second Anniversary Card. Dad either feels the war is nearing its end and therefore he'll be home soon to settle into domestic life or he just yearns for it so badly he's compelled to draw about it.

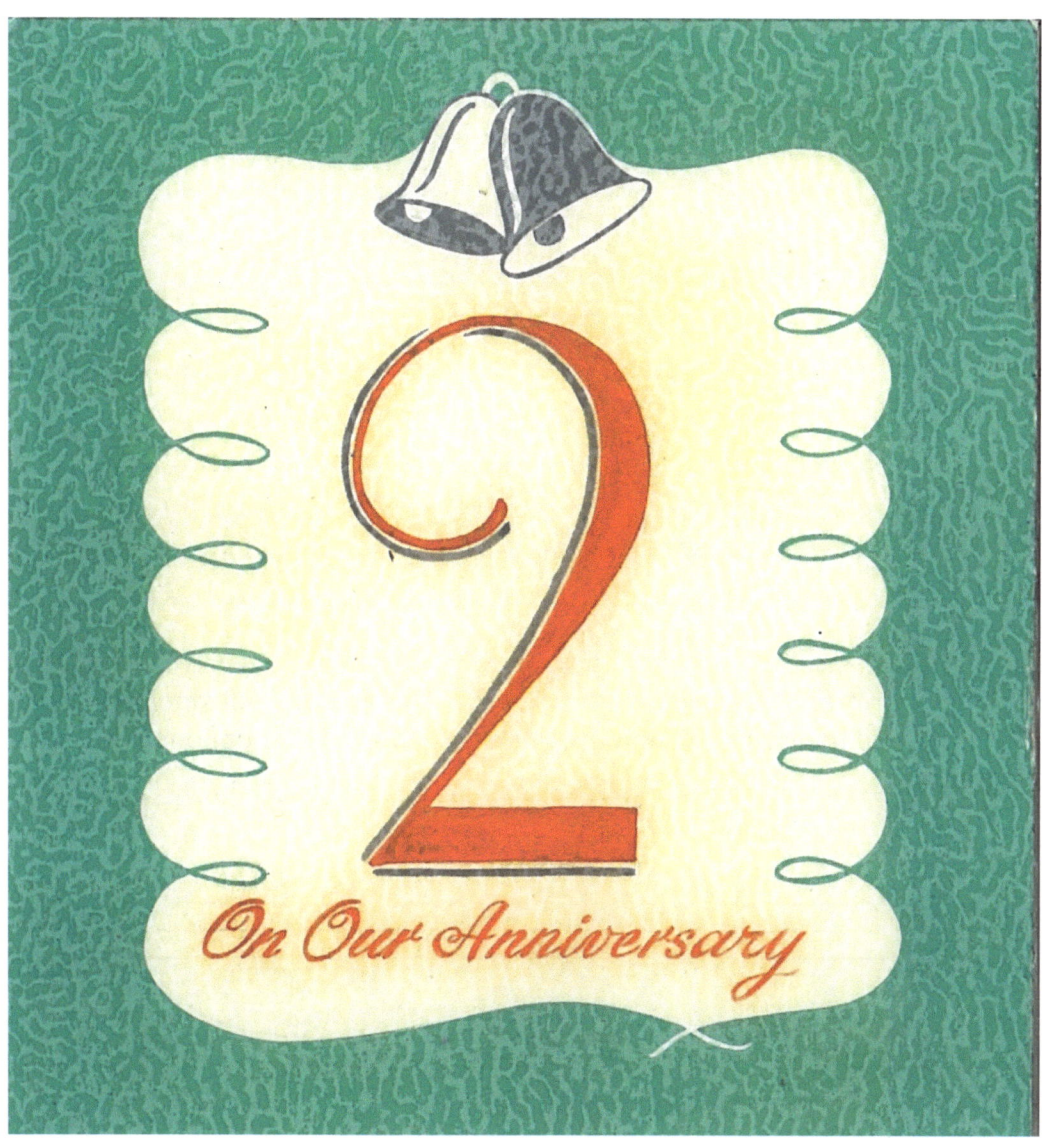

And before any 21st century people get all up in arms about my Mom doing dishes while my contented Dad idly stands by with his pipe, remember these were very different times. I can't say my Mom had fun doing the dishes though... we were one of the first families on our street to have an automatic dishwasher.

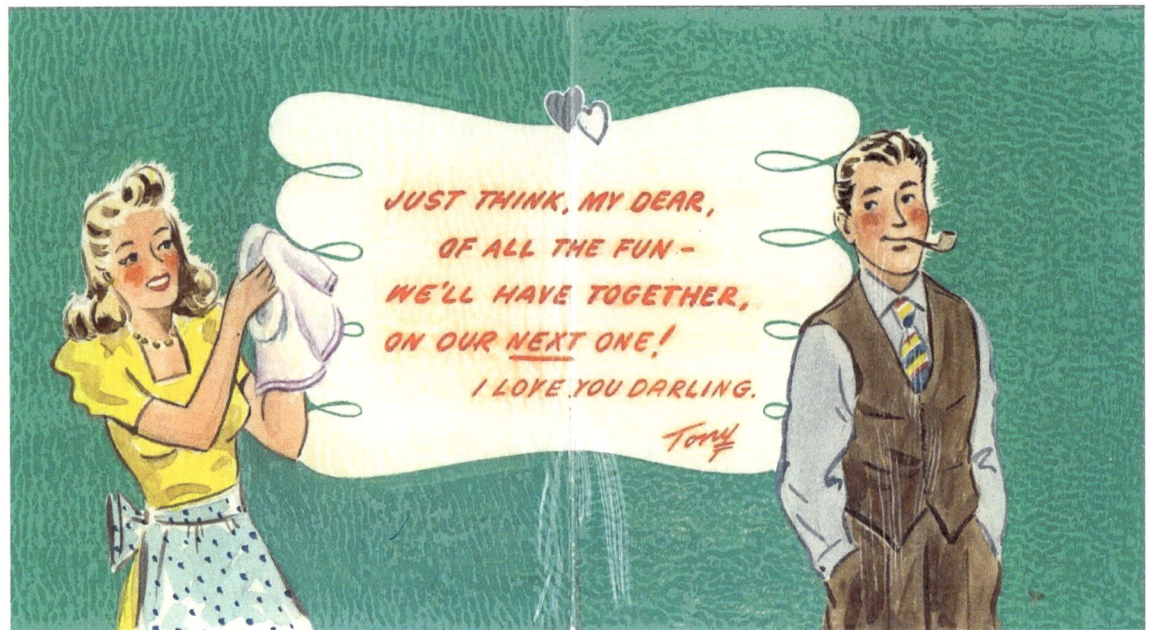

By the way, I never saw my Dad actually smoke a pipe but I can vaguely remember him smoking cigarettes (Viceroys) and then Tiparillo cigars. He quit smoking, probably in the mid to late 1960's and became a stanch and vocal opponent of any kind of smoking.

IL PROGRESSO ITALO-AMERICANO ARTICLE

We also have the good fortune of a newspaper article (thanks to my cousin Oscar) from the Italian-American newspaper *Il Progresso Italo-Americano*, showing my Dad with his Aunt Mary and Uncle John, who are Oscar's parents.

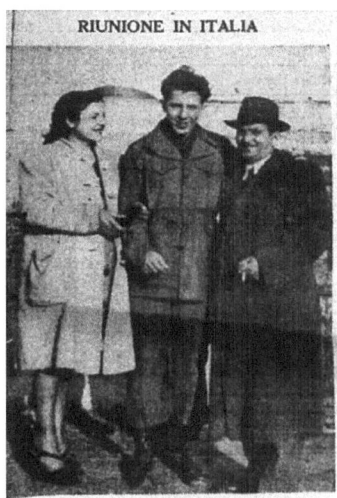

RIUNIONE IN ITALIA

Il Sergente Anthony Grande ritratto con gli zii Giovanni e Maria Masciandaro sulla terrazza della casa dei nonni a Gioia del Colle-Bari

Il Sergente Anthony Grande visita i nonni e numerosi parenti a Gioia del Colle

Soleri invoca revisione delle monetarie del

Translation: Reunion in Italy

Mr. and Mrs. Frank Grande, who reside at 206 West 36th Street, New York City have received a letter from their son - Sergeant Anthony W. Grande in which he describes his visit to Gioia del Colle, where he spent the Christmas holidays with his maternal grandparents Guiseppe and Clara Masciandaro, Joseph Masciandaro, Salvador and Dora Masciandaro, John and Mary Masciandaro, Gisseppe, Adelina and Leo Masciandaro, Camillo and Calestina Tangorra, Ottavio and Giannina Milano as well as with various cousins that he met for the first time. They all gave him care and attention to make the occasion even more enjoyable.

Due to transportation difficulties, he was not able to go to Toritto, birthplace of his father, where many of his paternal relatives live.

In his letter, the Sergeant Major informed his parents that the town of Gioia del Colle itself had suffered only very slightly from the effects of the war but adds that the population is struggling with heartrending misery and asks for aid from relatives and friends in America.

The Sergeant Major has obtained a diploma from Bryant High School and then studied at The Mechanics Institute on 5th Ave. and 44th Street, New York. He was called to arms in 1941. He was sent into the Mediterranean theater and took part in the invasion of Africa and Tunisia. He was one of the first to disembark at Salerno. He participated in the epic Battle of Cassino and was one of the first to enter Rome. He is currently located on the advanced lines with the troops of the Genius.

It is hoped that he will be soon return to his father and mother, Mr. Frank and Mariannina Grande and his wife Marian Grande in the United States after 29 months of absence.

Another son of Mr. Grande is Corporal Joe J. Grande, located with a department of bombers in England. During his off time, Corporal Grande prepares programs for his band. Corporal Grande distinguished himself in 200 aerial missions. He is the head of an orchestra that plays in the style of the famous Glen Miller Orchestra. Last August, an Allied airplane was shot down during a tragic flight from England to France. On that occasion, Corporal Grande received enthusiastic congratulations by Gen. Doolittle, the hero of the first flight against Japan. He has been in the service since February of 1943 and called to arms while a member of his father's orchestra.

The article suggests that I probably haven't given my Dad enough credit for the battle action he experienced. Regardless, I am proud of my Dad for serving in the war and protecting the freedoms we all enjoy to this day.

VALENTINE'S DAY 1944

Dad creates a beautiful card for this occasion. The Italian air must have filled him with romanticism as he is back to crafting poetry. This poem isn't bad. I think Mom would have loved this card.

Could this be an early 3-D card? If you stare into the red heart for a few seconds, it appears to float over the page. (The heart on the right demonstrates the effect a little better than the left.) Do you see it? Or am I wrong? I wonder if this effect was intentional.

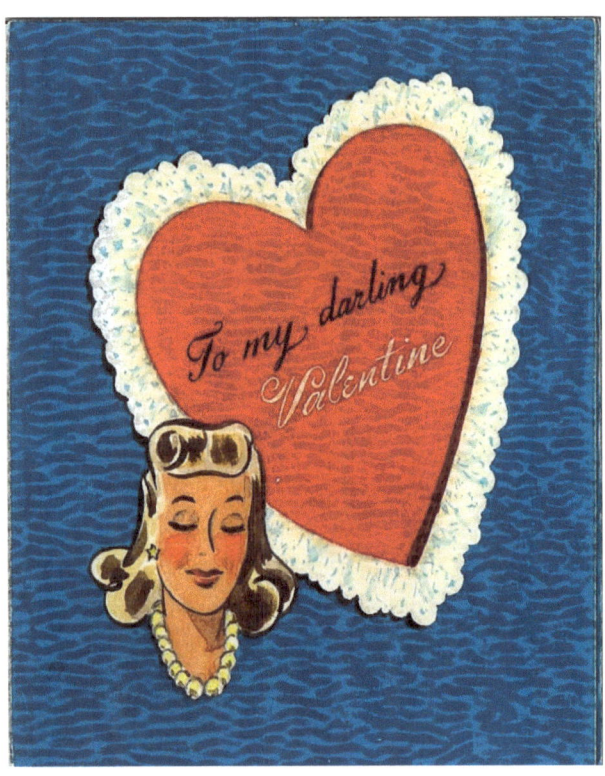
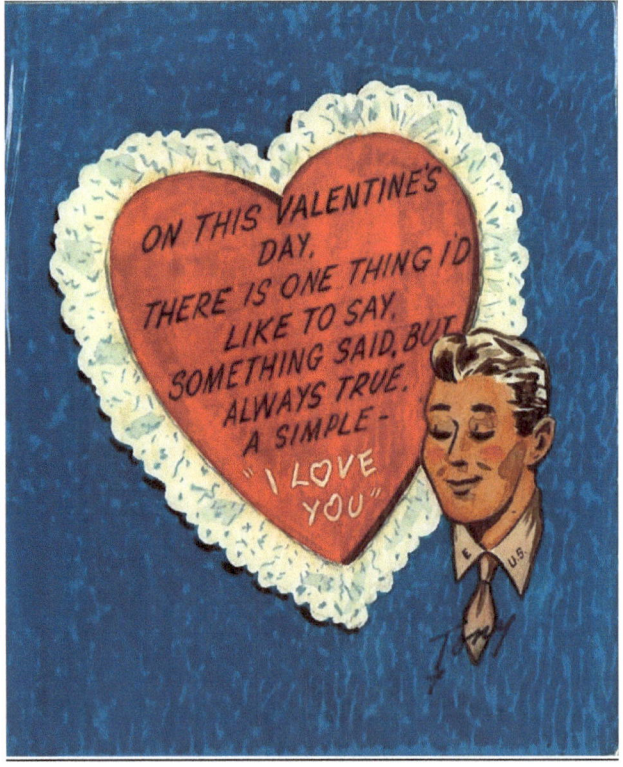

<u>FOR MOM'S 24th BIRTHDAY</u>

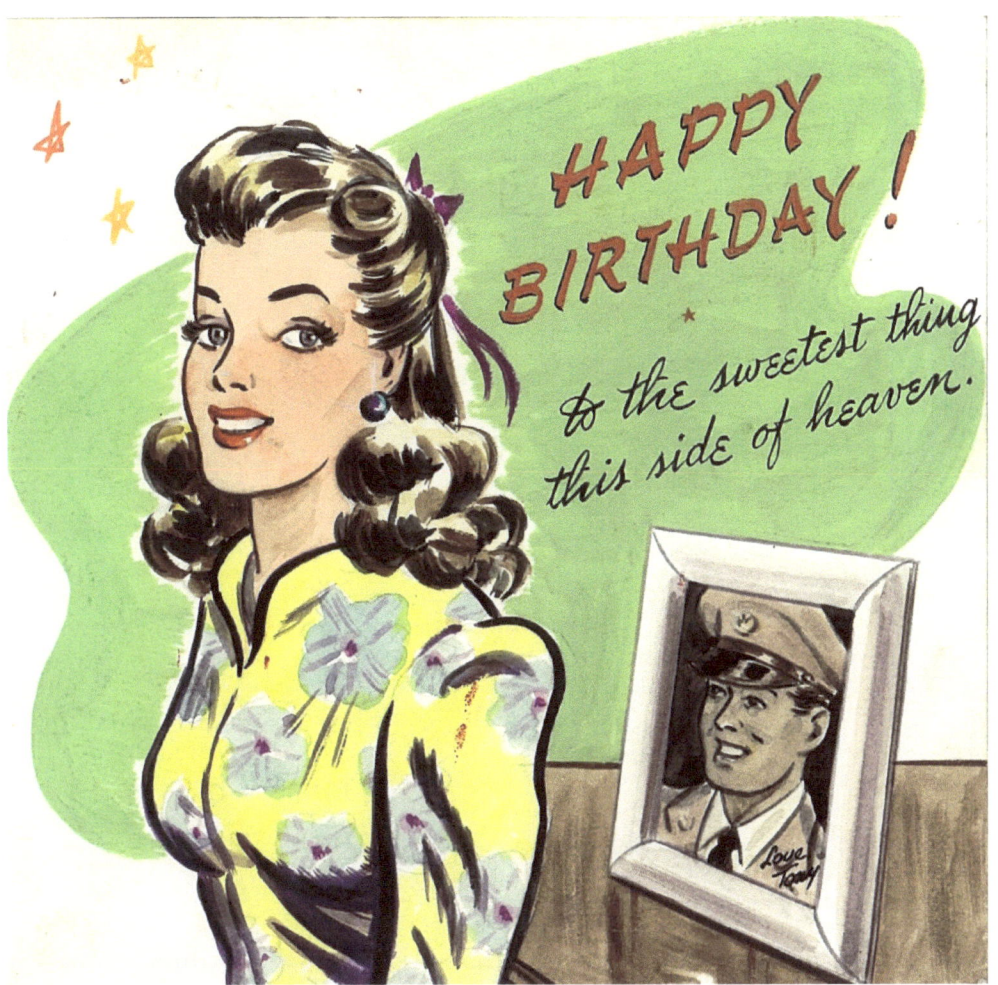

I love this card! It brings a smile to my face every time I see it. Mom definitely looks like "the sweetest thing this side of heaven!"

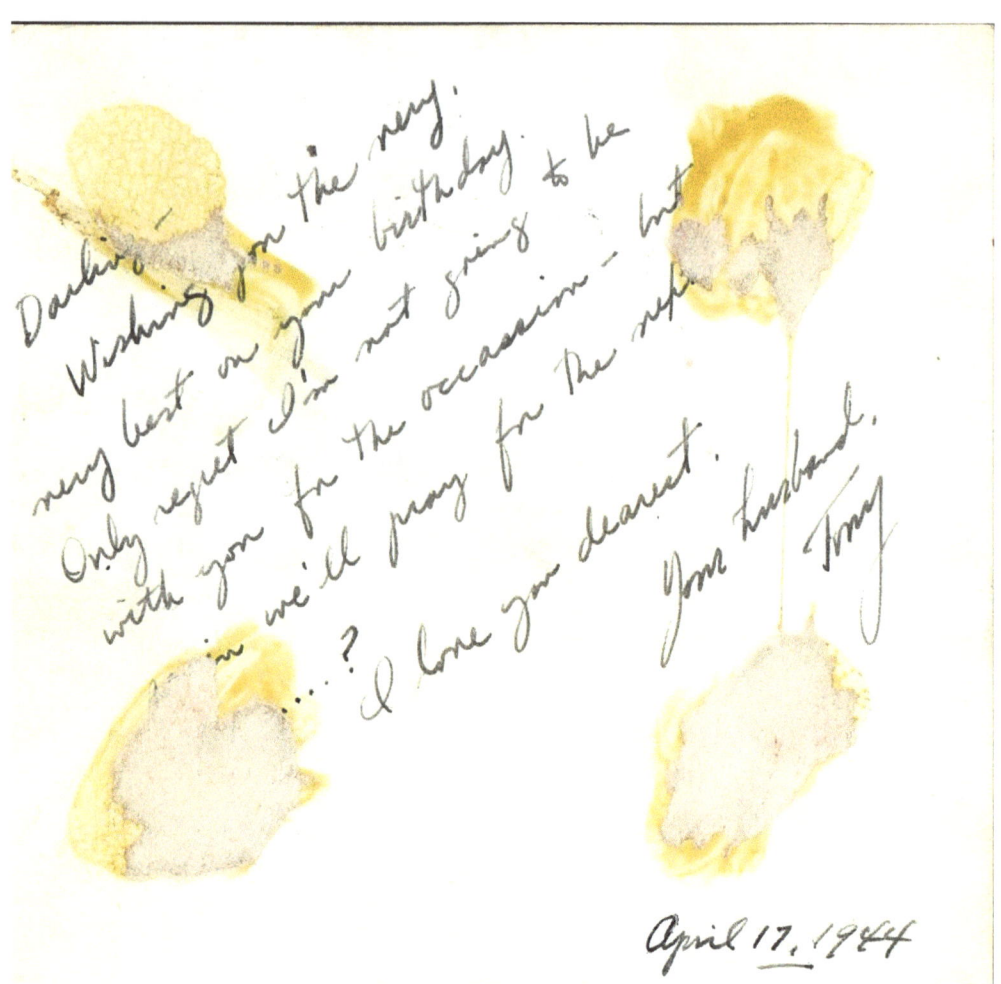

Darling—
Wishing you the very.
very best on your birthday.
Only regret I'm not going to be
with you for the occasion—but
...we'll pray for the ...
...?
I love you dearest.
Your husband.
Tony

April 17, 1944

And I love the thoughtful handwritten note on the back. (Excuse the glue residue.) There are more references to God and prayer here. I'm thinking that even a secular man in times of war embraces his higher power. Reading between the lines, he is obviously tired of the war and expected it to have ended by now.

CHRISTMAS 1944

It's Christmas time, 1944 and Dad doesn't disappoint. Dad, in a framed photo watches over Mom as she trims the tree. He has used this picture frame "creative trick" before.

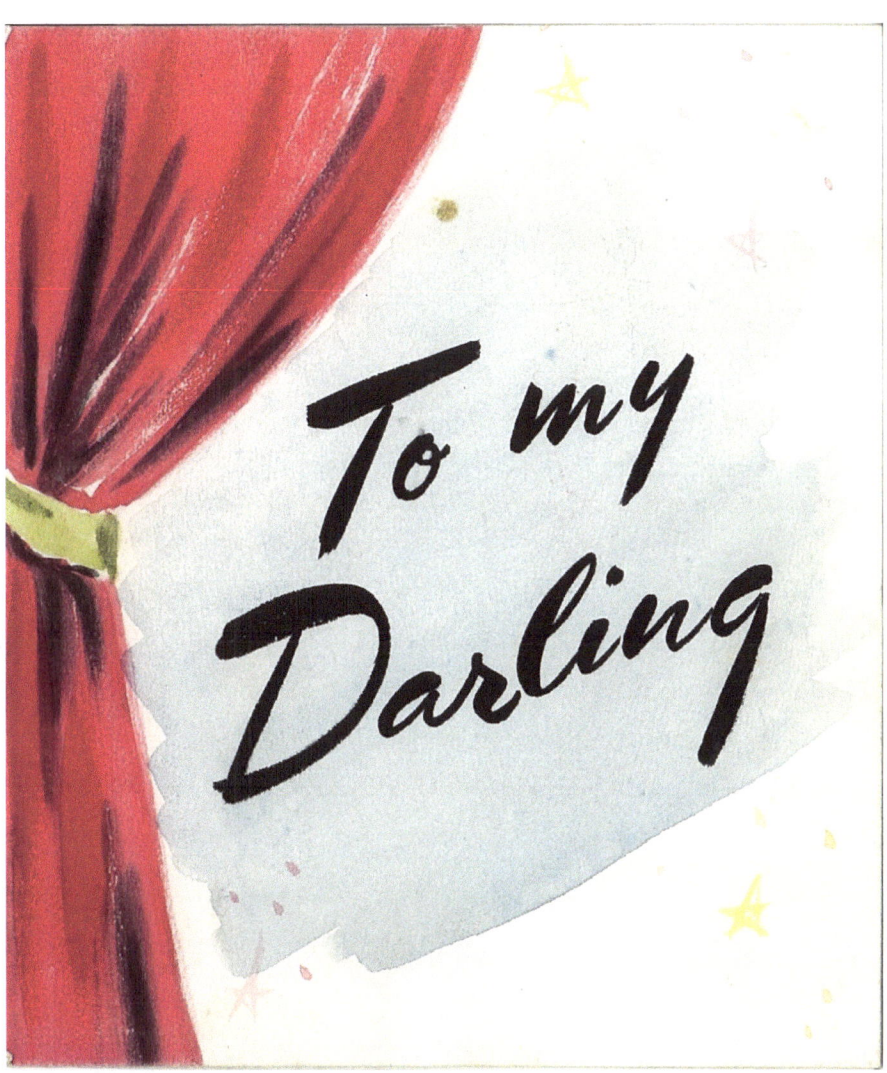

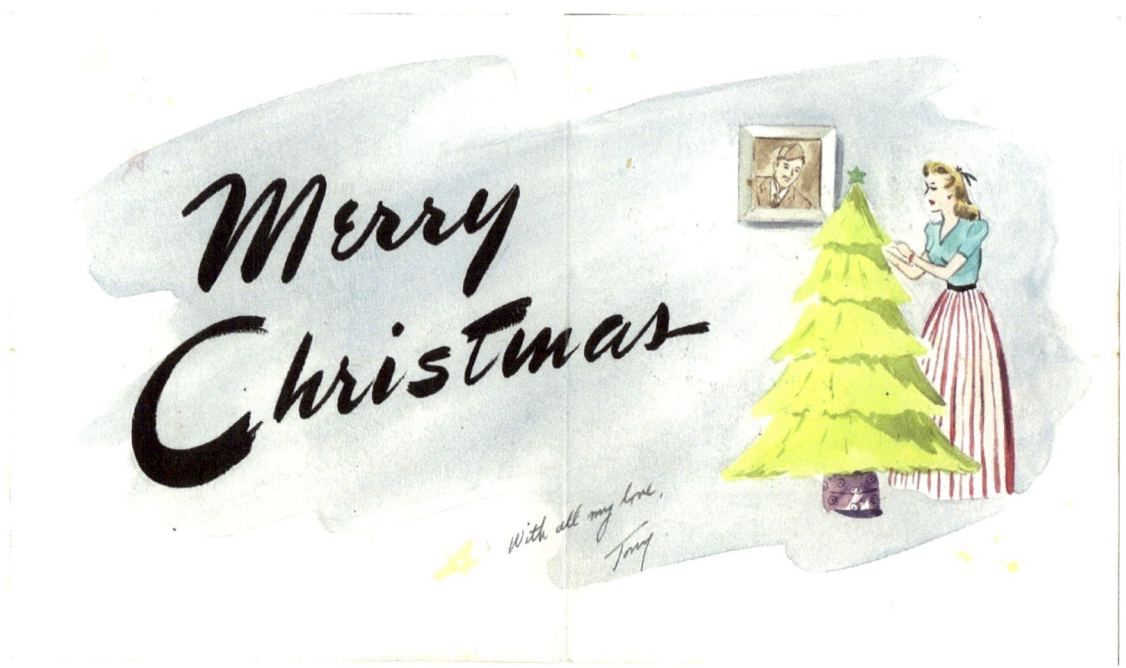

Dad writes a handwritten note on the back of the card that reads,

Hope this is the last card from overseas dear...
December 25, 1944

Yes! Finally... this IS the last Christmas card from overseas!!!!

VALENTINE'S DAY, 1945

It's Valentine's Day, 1945 and the war will be over in 6 months. Dad pledges his love to Mom "forever and ever" and conveys this thought by a series of repeating hearts that travel from (or to) infinity. Very clever I would say.

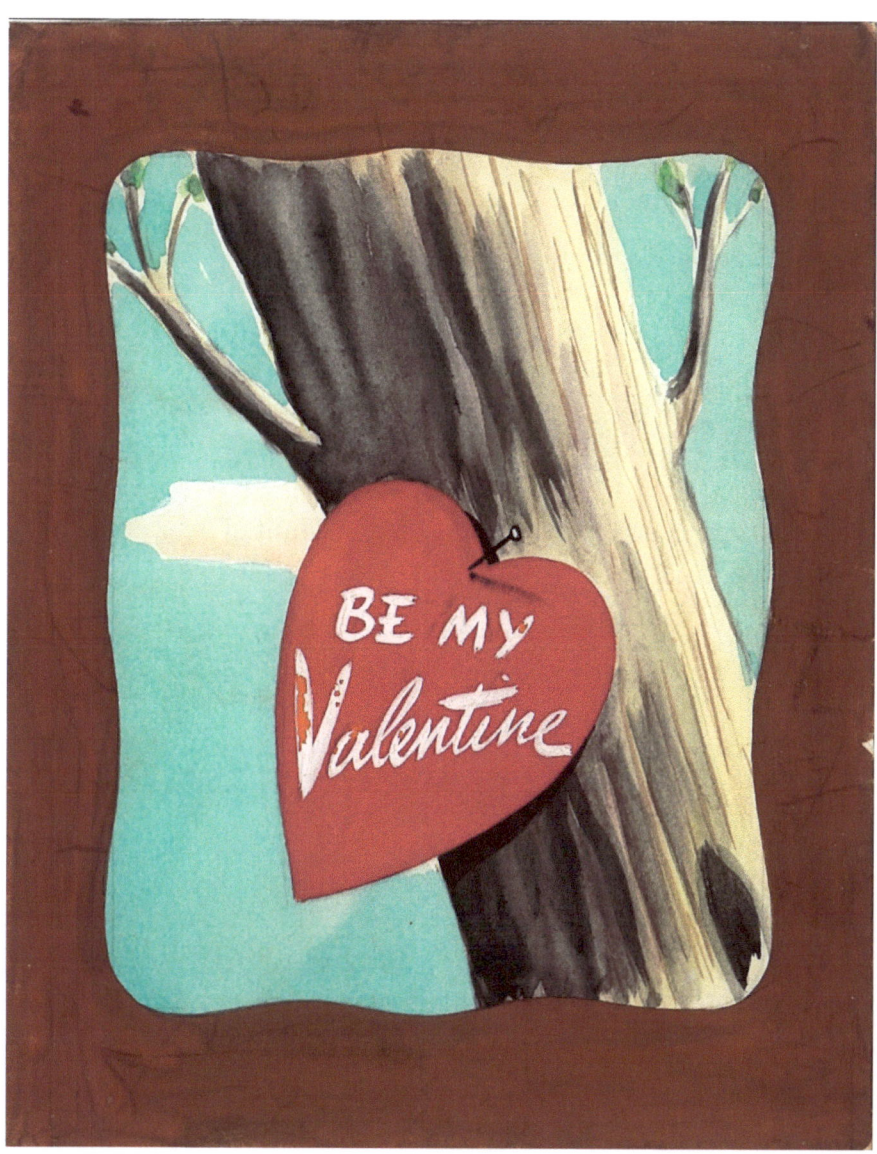

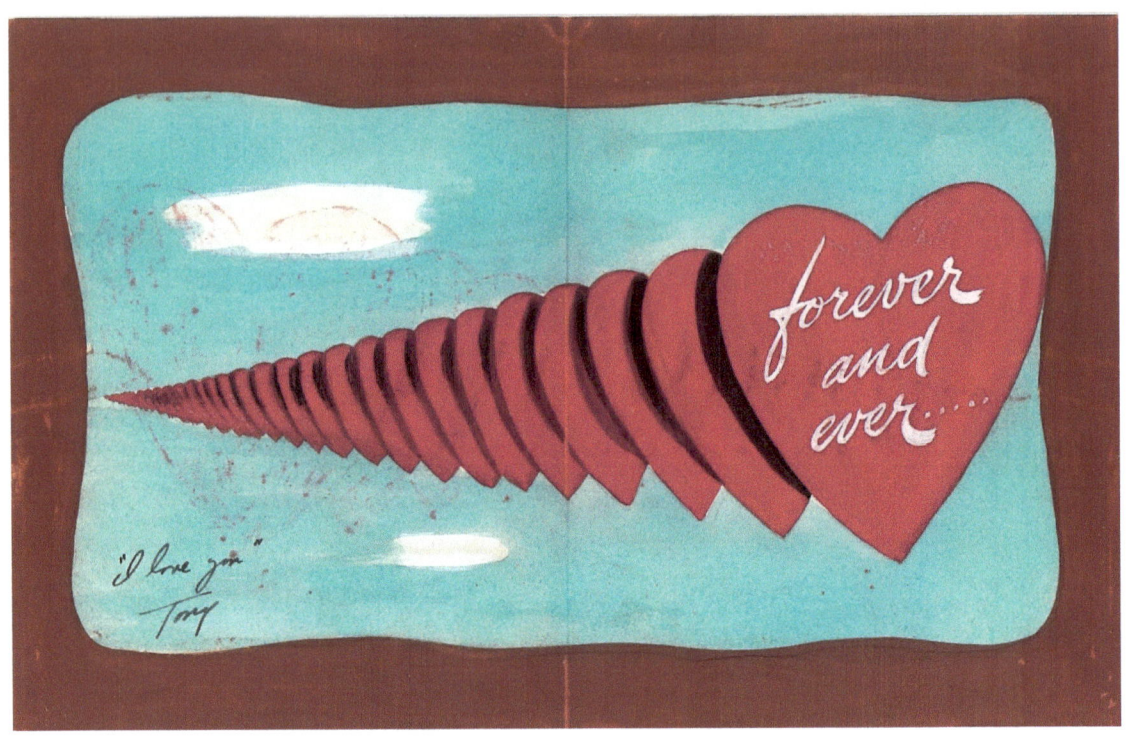

There are so many "forever and ever" hearts on this card! I counted over 40 before my eyes started hurting.

THEIR THIRD ANNIVERSARY

It's April 1945 and Dad is still stationed in Italy. I'm sorry to say that Mom and Dad's Third Anniversary wasn't enjoyed together "back in the states" as hoped or expected. But Dad will return home soon afterwards.

In this card, Dad puts himself back in uniform, smoking a pipe and thinking of Mom. As I mentioned earlier, Dad would tell us how much he disliked the army. He despised the regimentation.

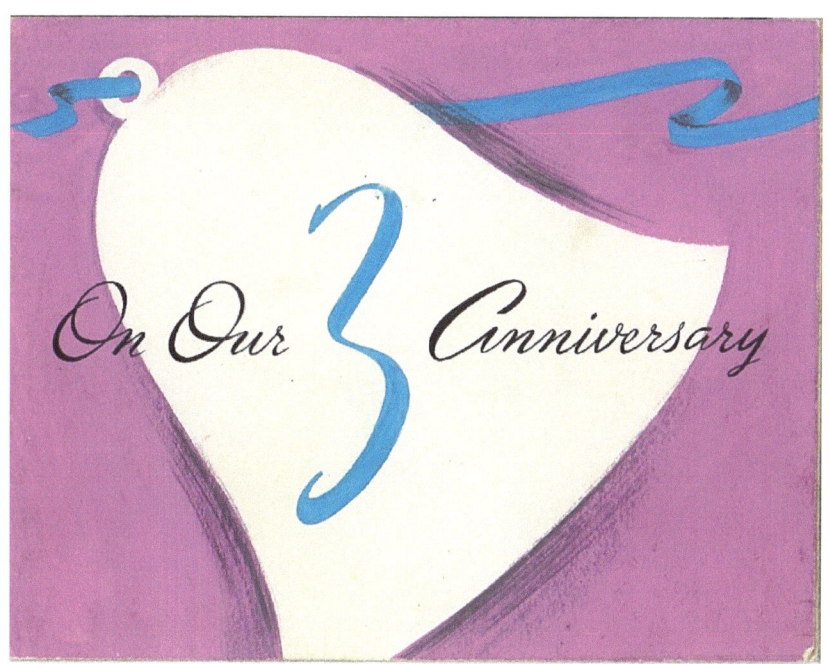

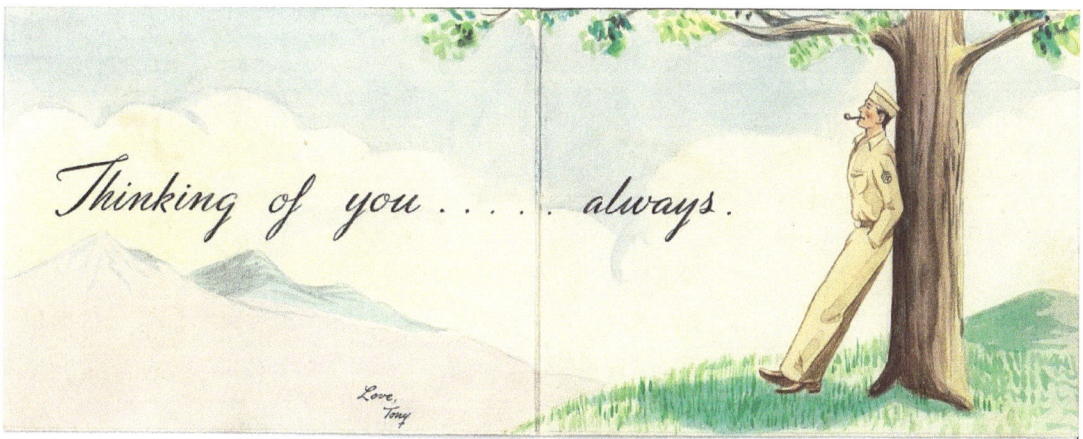

This Third Anniversary Card is fairly simple but that's the beauty of it. There's no reference to "hoping this is the last one from overseas." However, I would think the prevailing thought was that "the end was near."

And the war's end was in fact, nearing. April marks the month in which German forces surrendered in Italy. Hitler takes his own life in his underground bunker on April 30th. The world is infinitely better without him. Total and unconditional surrender was signed in May.

MOM'S BIRTHDAY 1945

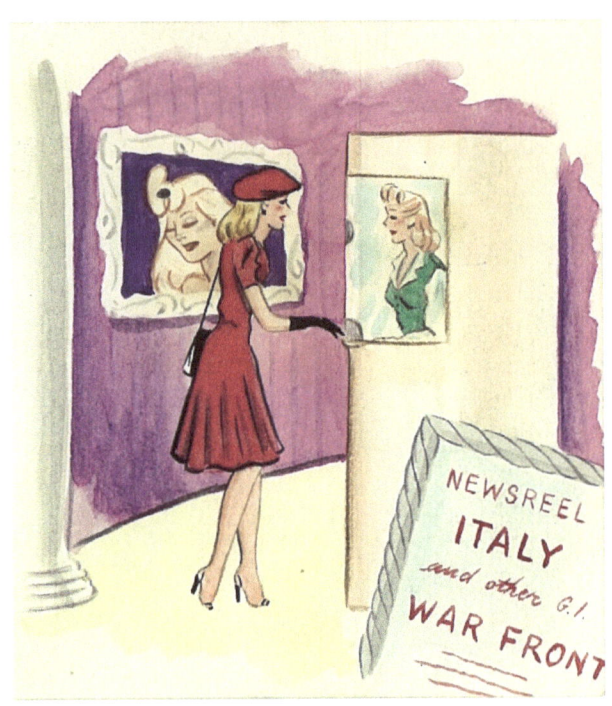

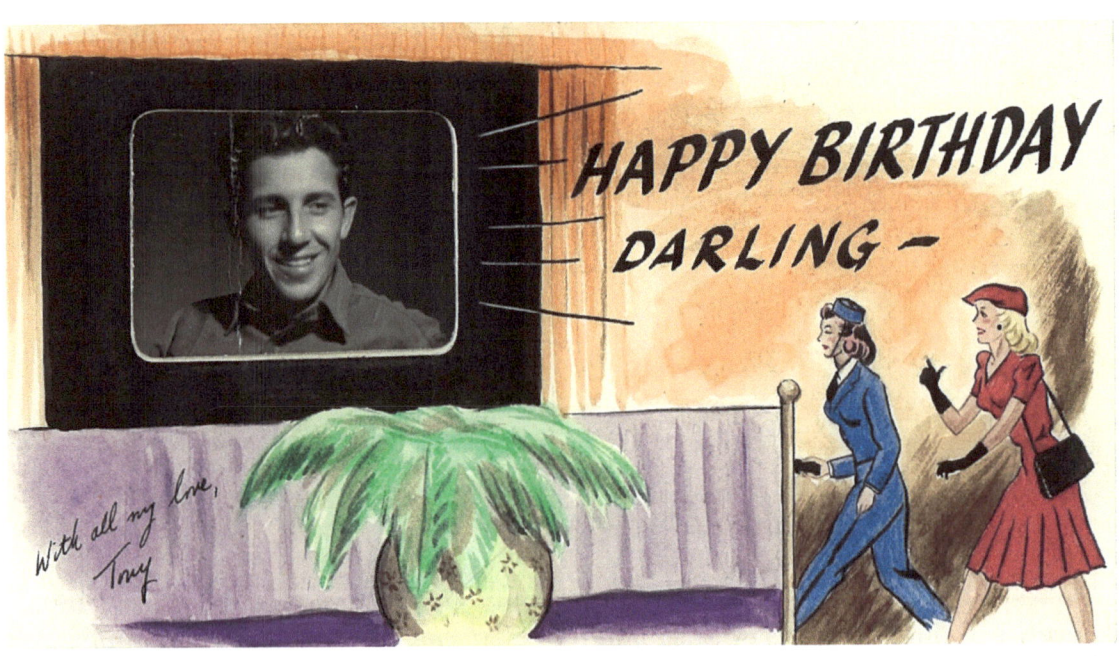

It's another very creative card featuring an actual photo of my Dad on the movie screen! Not sure why Mom has blond hair. Mom was always a brunette.

THE WAR IS OVER!

After the U.S. drops two atomic bombs on the cities of Hiroshima and Nagasaki, and the Soviet Union declares war on the Empire of Japan (the final Axis Power), Emperor Hirohito announces their surrender on August 15, 1945. The surrender is officially signed on September 2, V-J Day. THE WAR IS OVER!

I wish we had at least one more card announcing to Mom that he would be seeing her soon... It was obviously a glorious time for the Allies and for Americans both home and abroad.

Being apart for so long had to be agonizing. And the chance that they may never see each other again must have been almost unbearable. I can only imagine the sheer joy of reuniting!

POST WAR AND MISCELLANEOUS

There's a little mystery to this 1946 Christmas Post-War Card, as there is a note missing from the card. The note explains "something that happened to him" which is a reason for something that Dad "didn't do." Buy the right gift? Buy a gift at all? Did he buy too many gifts to bring home all at once? (My 3rd guess is a just a joke.)

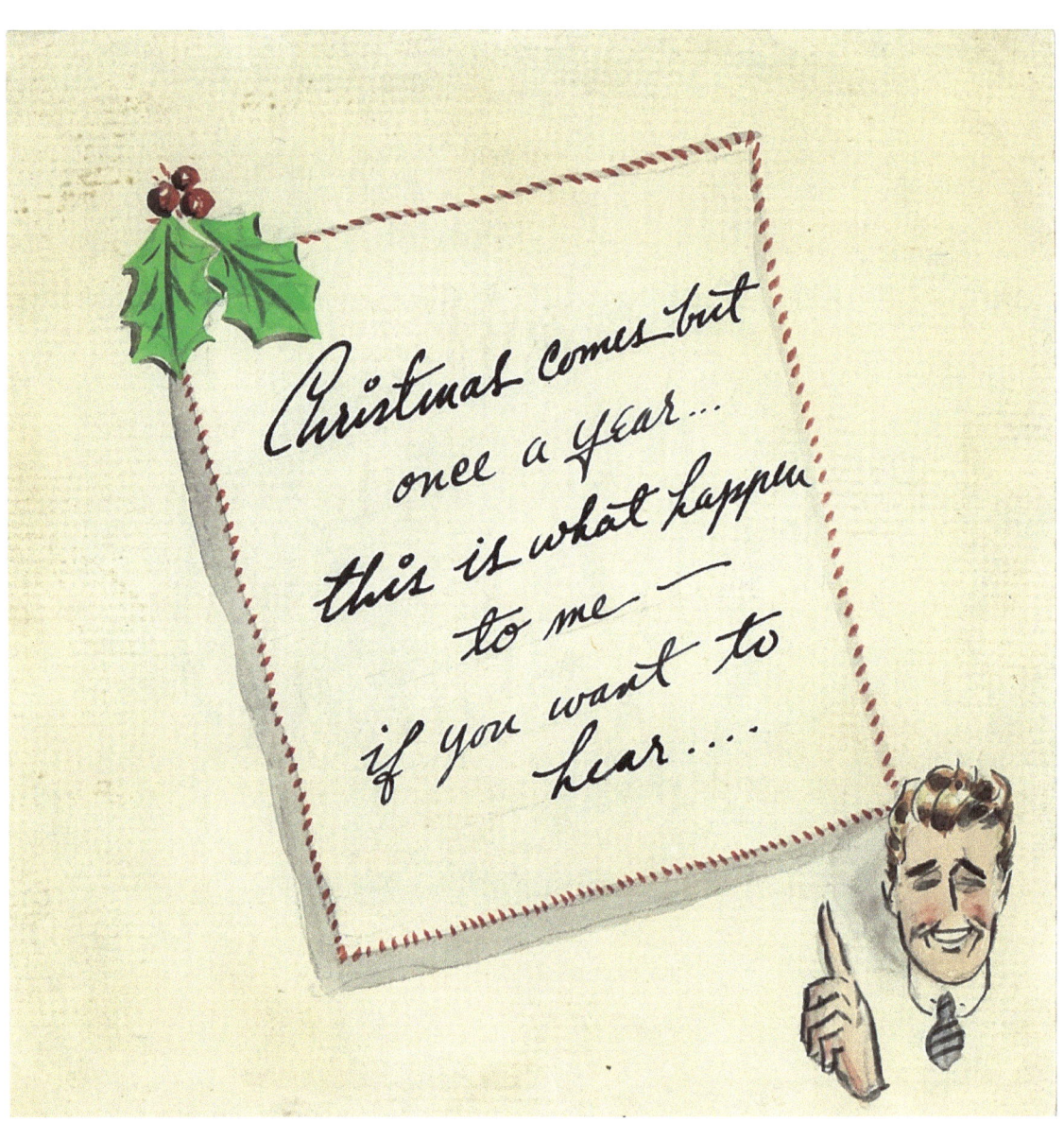

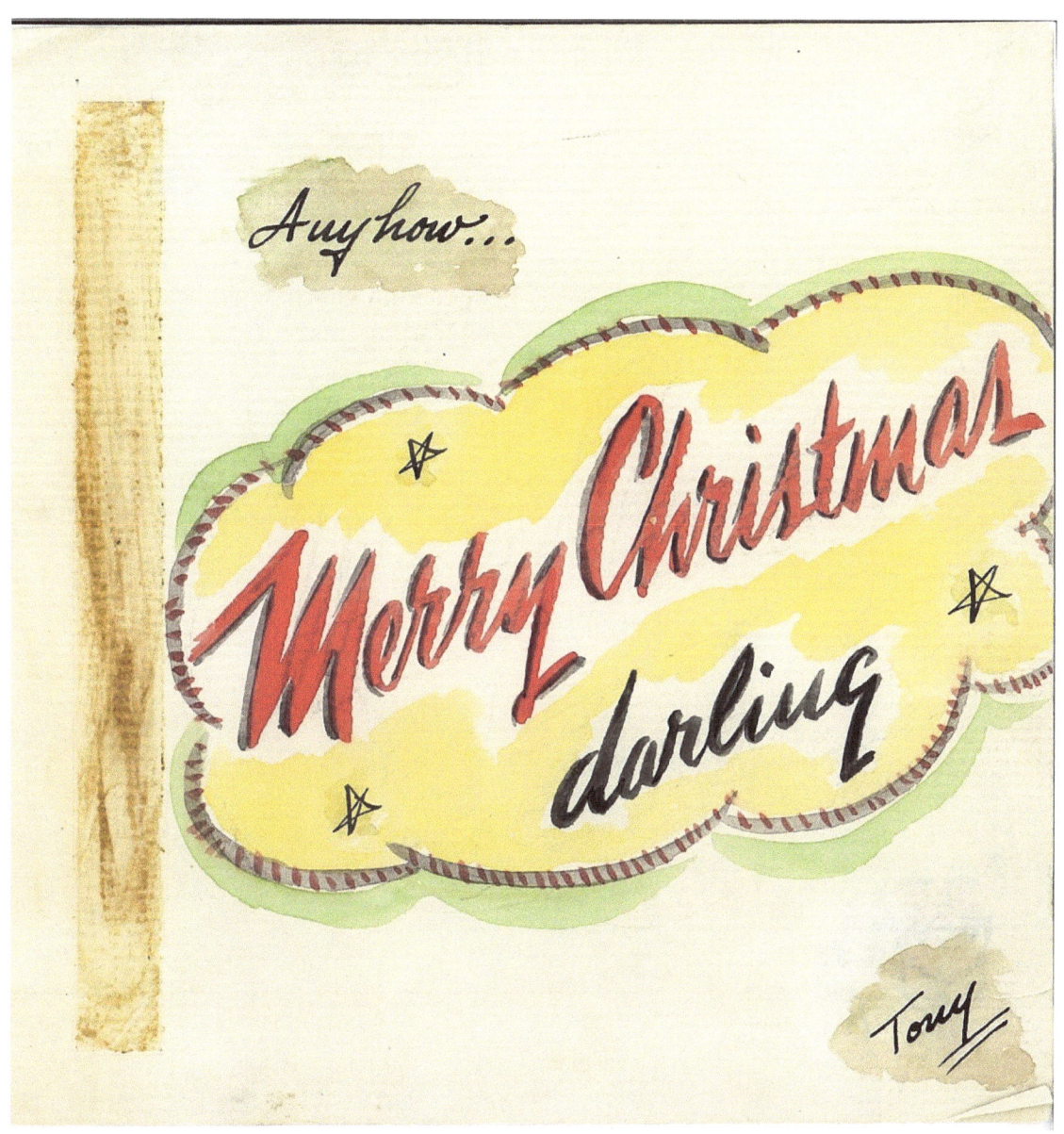

Dad must have glued the note to the inside. I'm betting Dad didn't buy a Christmas present for Mom (again). I could joke and say Mom pulled the note off the page, ripped it up and threw it in Dad's face but... that's not my Mom's nature. She most likely laughed and gave Dad a huge hug and kiss. Mom would usually let him off the hook fairly easily.

FILL HER UP!

This is probably an idea of Dad's for a promotional piece he had in mind for an oil company like… ESSO. (Dad went on to have a successful career as a Creative Director in advertising. Think "Mad Men.") By the way, how many of us remember when EXXON was ESSO? I'd guess very few.

When you opened the "card", the car moves so happily down the country road (aided by a slit in the card stock). ESSO should have bought the idea. Come to think of it, are there any EXXON marketing executives reading this?

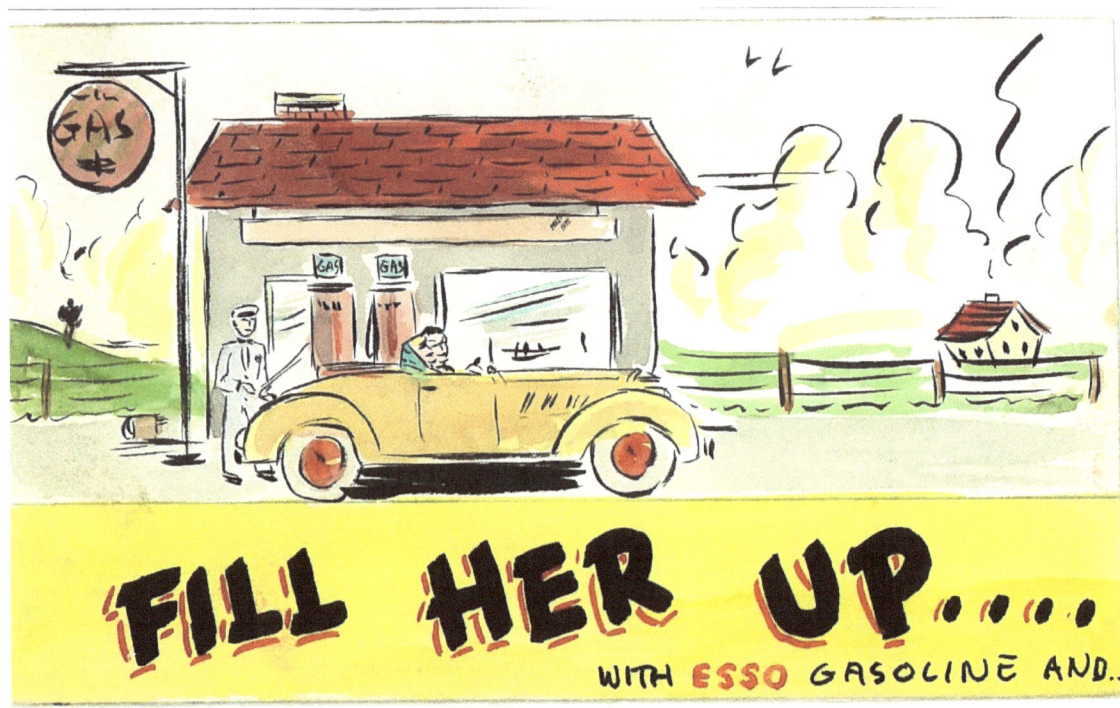

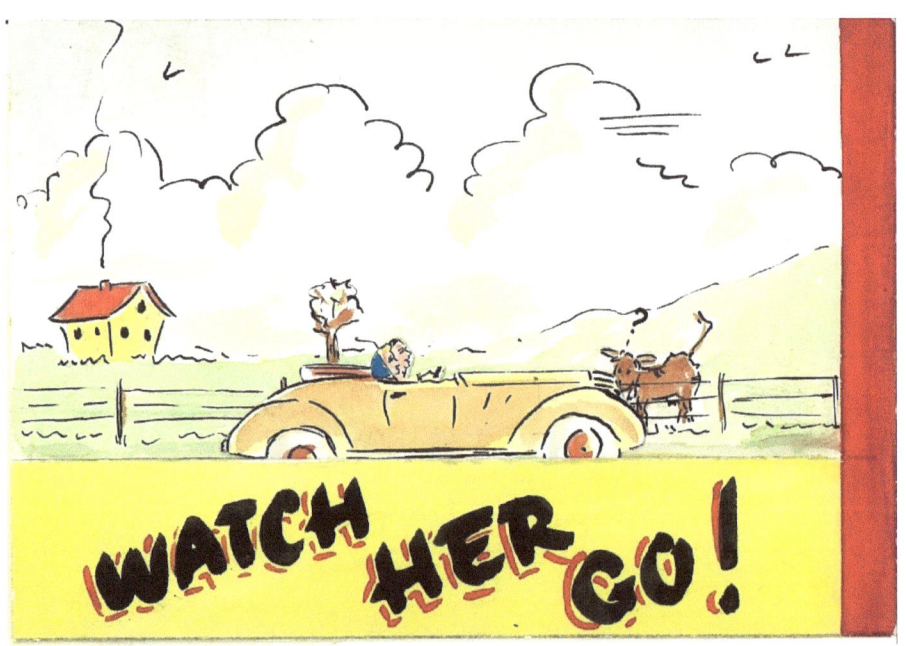

<u>MOM IN PROFILE</u>

This drawing does indeed look like Mom back in her 20's. And she did a lot of smiling in her lifetime.

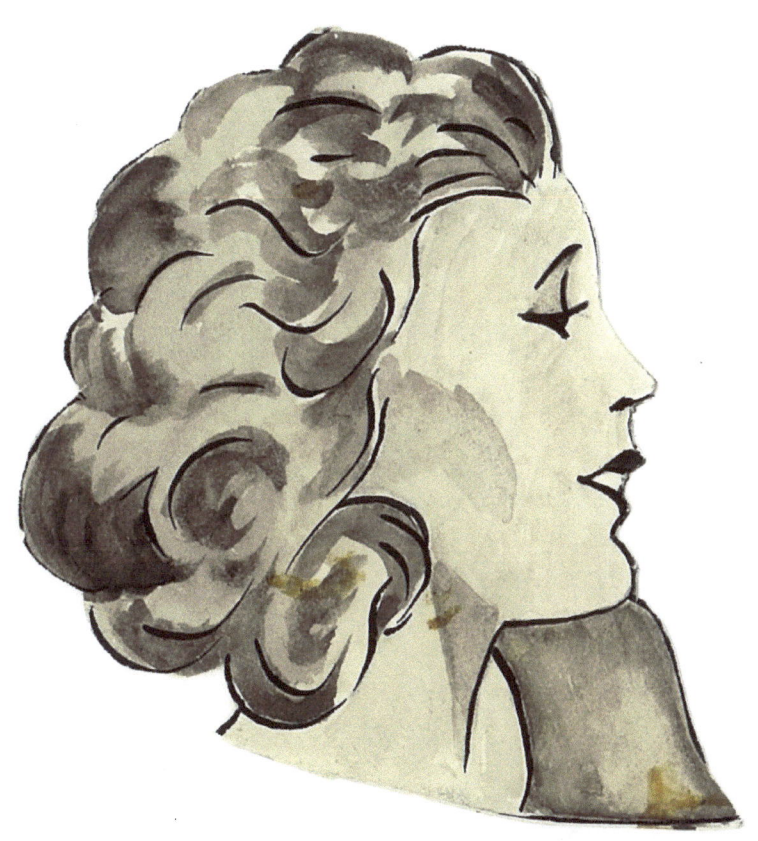

THE OLD LADY AND THE BUTCHER

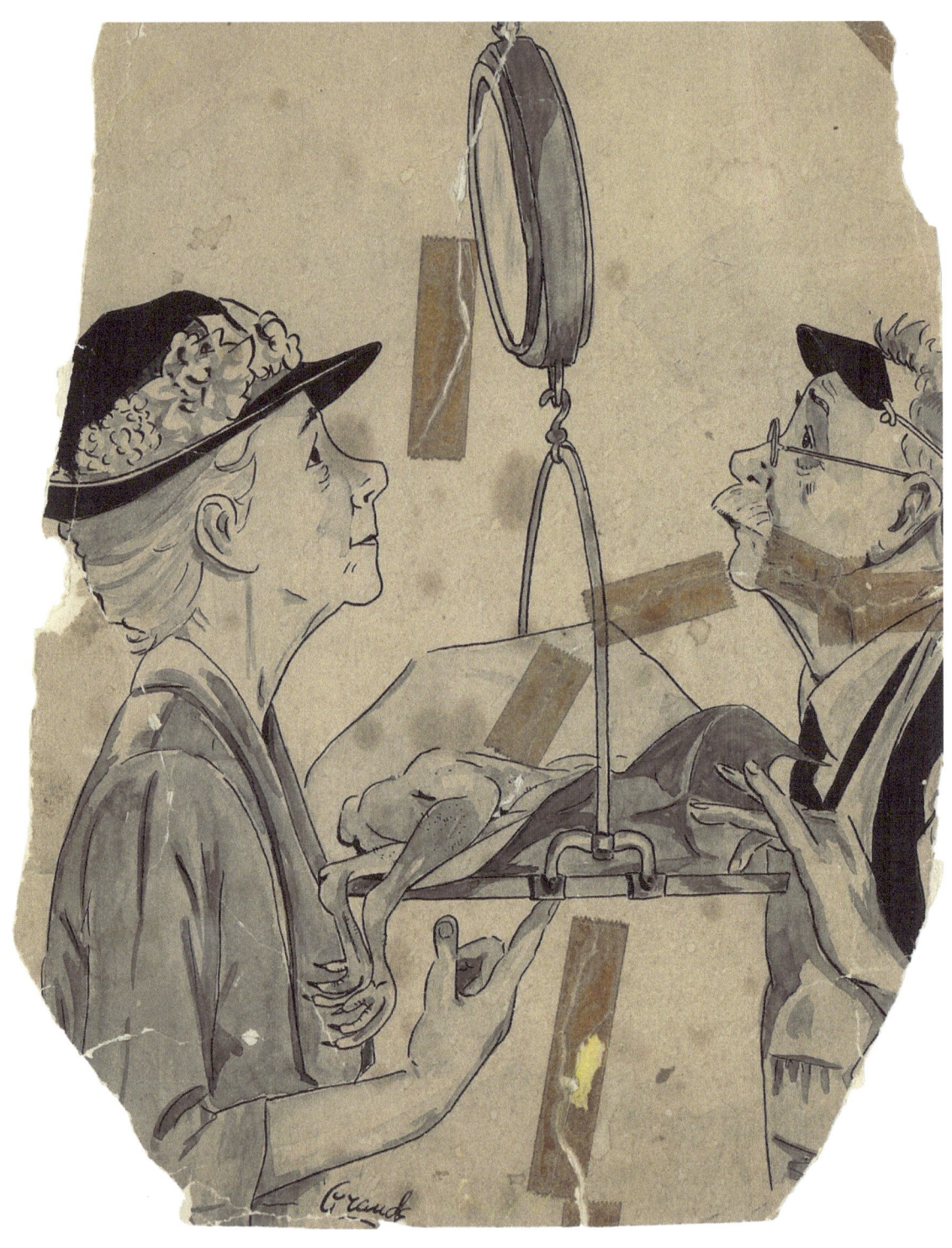

This black and white drawing is so beat up! It could just as well have gone to war with Dad. The characters in this drawing are both "cheaters" but they are so innocent looking, you couldn't be mad at them. Everyone must have been counting his or her pennies… literally, back then.

I'm not sure if the "Old Lady and The Butcher" concept is an original idea --- I thought it could very well have been a copy of a Norman Rockwell piece but I checked the Rockwell catalogue and there's nothing I found that is similar --- but it wouldn't matter to me either way. It is drawn so beautifully and precisely.

WANTCHA MADNESS

This next piece was sent to Mom sometime during Dad's military stint. There's no way to find the exact date so I decided to include this card in this section. The footnote claims it was taken from a poem in the military newspaper, "The Stars and Stripes." My research was unable to find the poem in its original form. I love the little "Army Guy".

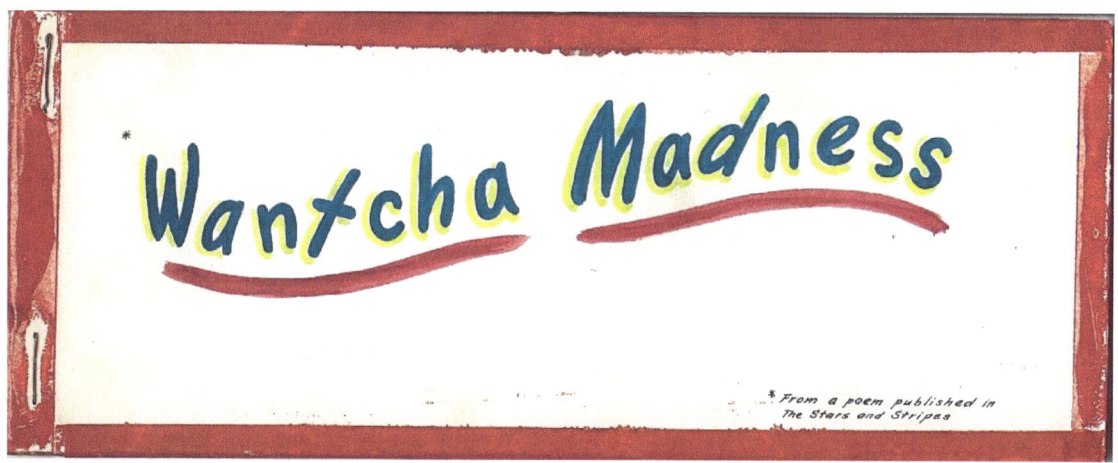

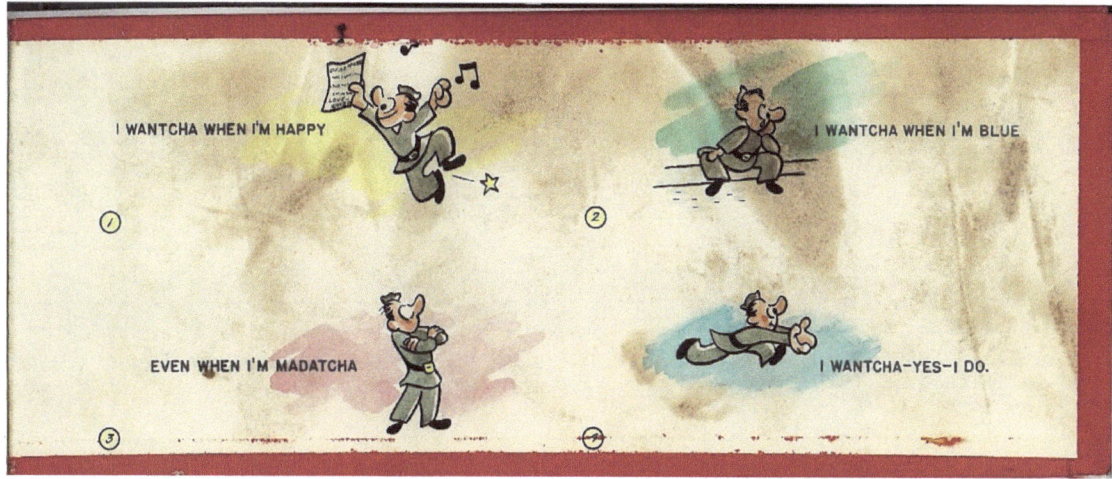

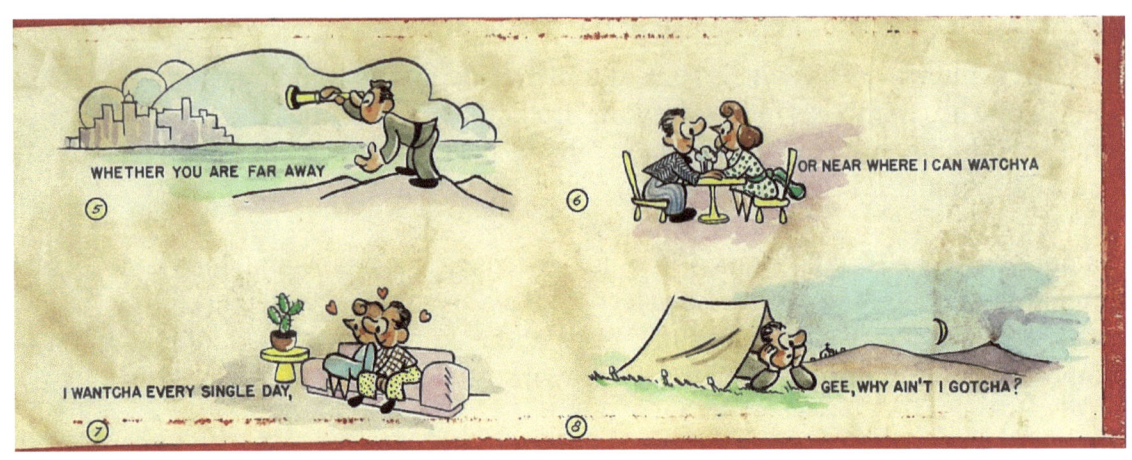

THE CLOSING BELL A.K.A THE WEDDING BELL

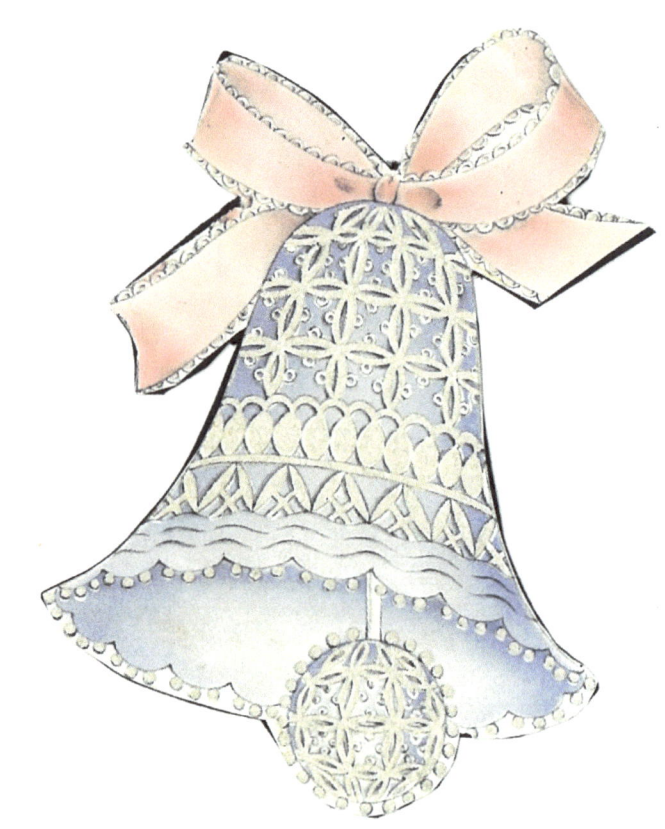

This ornate bell at one time was affixed to something wedding related... but whatever it was is long gone --- unlike all the wonderful memories and discoveries that the work on this book have given me.

All the hours of work I put into this book were well worth the effort. You might say this undertaking was a "labor of love." I gained a new insight and perspective about Mom and Dad by virtue of researching this book.

I gained confirmation that they both greatly loved and appreciated life. Growing up during the depression and living through the war will have that effect, I suppose. And the "Boom" years after the war must have been a great era in which to live. "Whew, we made it through," people must have thought to themselves.

I'll make just one final mention about the relationship between my Mom and Dad. I can only recall ONE TIME when they had an argument. I remember finding Mom in her bedroom crying and only then realized something was up. But I don't remember the "fight" lasting much longer beyond that.

Is it "normal" not to fight at least a little more often? It was perfectly normal for my Mom and Dad.

WHAT'S NEXT

Depending upon the degree of success this book enjoys, I may publish the catalogue of original Holiday Cards my Dad designed, had printed and sent out (by Mom and us kids).

Please send me your thoughts, comments and questions. I'm at rick.grande52@gmail.com. I sincerely hope you enjoyed my Mom and Dad's love story.